D1553479

MONEY AND FICTION

By the same author:

The Garden and the Map: Schizophrenia in Twentieth-Century Literature and Culture

Ann

Poetry and the Body

Money and Fiction

Literary Realism in the Nineteenth and Early Twentieth Centuries

John Vernon

Cornell University Press

ITHACA AND LONDON

First published 1984 by Cornell University Press.
Published in the United Kingdom by
Cornell University Press Ltd., London.

International Standard Book Number 0-8014-1728-7
Library of Congress Catalog Card Number 84-12166
Printed in the United States of America
Librarians: Library of Congress cataloging information
appears on the last page of the book.

The paper in this book is acid-free and meets the guidelines
for permanence and durability of the Committee on Production
Guidelines for Book Longevity of the Council on Library Resources.

Contents

Preface

Money and Fiction examines the realistic novel from the opening decades of the nineteenth century to about 1900, though the Introduction touches upon the early novel (Defoe and Fielding) and the Epilogue upon the modern novel (Wharton, Dreiser, and Gide). I use the theme of money—perhaps the most common theme in nineteenth-century fiction—as a prism with which to separate and examine such elements as narrative time, plot, and the representation of material objects, all of which are formal expressions of the novel's social and economic context. Along the way, my most persistent intention is to examine and analyze the various ways the realistic novel does and does not represent reality, and my most persistent analogy is the comparison between the novel's claim to represent reality and paper money's claim to represent things of (presumably) enduring value: gold and silver. Like the nineteenth-century novel, paper money is a fiction with its roots in the actual—but a fiction nonetheless.

I am tempted to term this book an archaeology of ideas, but my approach is both more metaphoric and more eclectic than that of the acknowledged master of such studies, Michel Foucault. The Introduction discusses in detail issues of method and scope; only now, however, when I see the book as a whole and perceive the trajectory it traces can I pinpoint my

Preface

subject: the dialectical relationship between fiction and reality. In the nineteenth century this relationship was mediated by society; hence the novel of manners. But from its beginning, the novel of manners found itself subverted by a reductive sense of material reality that perpetually threatened to reveal social differences as hard-won illusions. The first stirrings of this sense of things occurs in Jane Austen's *Persuasion*, which consequently appears in this book as a remote headwater of the modern novel. In *Persuasion*, a social change of profound significance for nineteenth- and twentieth-century culture can be glimpsed in embryo, a change that centers upon conceptions of wealth. As we shall see, by the nineteenth century wealth had come to be thought of not in terms of the security of a landed estate, but in terms of the pursuit of personal ambitions associated with expanding capital. And this change entailed an entirely new conception of material reality, one in which the bulk and quantity and sheer physical *presence* of objects—commodities with price tags—first entered fiction. From *Persuasion* through the great realist novels of the nineteenth century to the novels of Sartre and Beckett in our own century, with their visions of reality as an unredeemed physical surplus, fiction runs in a single channel, eroding its own social base.

Thus, as we shall see some two hundred pages from here, the twentieth century possesses far less claim to be called the age of money than does the nineteenth. The evidence is there in novels, and in the way those novels register the historical forces that speak through them. The love of money is not equivalent to what we today call (in the ethical sense) materialism—the love of objects and commodities for their own sake—though the love of money is its preparation, its necessary condition. In the nineteenth century money flares up as a force in itself, an autonomous power with its own inscrutable will; but in the twentieth century it becomes absorbed into the material flow of life, with which it is often confused. Indeed, money in the age of computers has become more and more a

8

residue of transactions, of instantaneous bookkeeping. Its source of value may still be labor, but its face has almost become obliterated. In our age, money as a representation tends to disappear into what it represents: forms of power on the one hand and the accumulation of commodities on the other. For the great modern writers, as a consequence—for Joyce, Gide, Proust, Kafka, Mann, and Beckett especially—the novel was an isolated effort of will and cunning, an individual, even Nietzschean, achievement. By contrast, in the nineteenth century to write fiction was not so much to aspire as to tap into a current of inventive possibilities created by the conditions of the society. Among these conditions, money was preeminent: it was more visible, more familiar—though new and strange too—and more insistent than it is today, both as reality and as dream, as wealth and as the absence of wealth. Even a cursory glance at the nineteenth-century novel reveals money to be that novel's most habitual obsession. Money registers the altered sense of reality that is realism's subject and at the same time enables us to understand the forms of representation realism evolved to record that subject.

I am grateful to the State University of New York, which awarded me a summer grant, and to SUNY Binghamton, which awarded me a research semester; both helped me to complete this book. Earlier versions of two chapters have appeared in periodicals: chapter 4 in the *Kenyon Review* (Fall 1982) and chapter 3 in the *ABC's of Reading* (Spring 1984).

JOHN VERNON

Binghamton, New York

MONEY AND FICTION

INTRODUCTION

Picking Pockets

Characters in novels ask embarrassing questions. How will he get the money he needs? Who will be her heir? Did he (or she) take the money, the jewels, the check, the handkerchief? Trollope can squeeze nine hundred pages out of such questions, as he does in both *The Last Chronicle of Barset* and *The Eustace Diamonds.* But more than a century before Trollope the profits of theft were limited by existing material conditions. For example, for pickpockets to flourish, first, men must possess pockets, and second, the money in those pockets must be both transferable and convertible. Thus, at the dawn of paper money in the late seventeenth century, we find Defoe's Colonel Jack unable to spend most of the money he and his friends steal from their victims' pockets because it comes in the form of large goldsmith's notes on which payment can easily be stopped. They do manage to exchange a smaller note for gold coins, but with problematic results for fifteen-year-old Jack, who finds that he—unlike his victims—has no pockets to keep his money in.

Colonel Jack sleeps in the ashes at the glass house, without a mattress, box, or drawer to hide his spoils in, with no floorboards to pry up. To this point he has lived in a world without money, a world in which he survives by running errands for merchants in exchange for food or clothing—in a barter economy. His expulsion from the garden of poverty occurs when he finds his fist full of gold guineas and has no place to put them: "And now as I was full of Wealth, behold! I was full of Care, for what to do to secure my Money I could not tell, and this held me so long, and was so Vexatious to me the next Day, that I truly sat down and cryed." That night he can't sleep, clinging to his gold, and the next morning he hides his money in a hole in a tree at the edge of town, only to watch it fall through the soft moss inside and disappear. This nightmarish scene is one of the most emotionally charged and strangely humorous passages in all of Defoe. Jack spends hours trying to retrieve the money before he finally wanders around the tree and discovers that the entire back is hollow and the money is lying there before him. He picks it up, cries out and dances, fondling and kissing the coins in an ecstasy of possession.

Then he undergoes two rites of passage. He buys pants with pockets, and immediately his guilt and worry are erased. "I gave her two Shillings for the Breeches, and went over into the Churchyard and put them on, put my Money into my new Pockets, and was as pleas'd as a Prince is with his Coach and six Horses. . . . I Was but a Boy, 'tis true, but I thought my self a Man now I had got a Pocket to put my money in." Later that day he goes to a gentleman who holds the money for him and gives him a note for it, a note of the same mystifying kind he had stolen and cashed. If P = paper and G = gold, we can characterize this exchange (in a variation of Marx's formula on commodities)[1] as $P \rightarrow G \rightarrow P'$, where P' represents the paper money that now is Jack's own, is negotiable for him, and even earns interest. Thus a key has been found; magic has occurred: paper not only can stand for gold, it can create more of it. Jack has found a magic pocket like the inexhaustible ones in

[1]See *Capital*, trans. Samuel Moore and Edward Aveling (New York: International Publishers, 1967), 1:154–155.

fairy tales—a bank. It really is, as Marx said, alchemy[2] or, in our own idiom, voodoo economics. And it turns out to be far more profitable than stealing. But for Jack, initially, it works only in small amounts. He can't cash large notes without raising suspicions, so must rely on money come by as a reward for returning the purses he steals. Thirty years later, however, in *Tom Jones* (about 1750), bank notes appear to be easier to cash. But Black George, finding the five hundred pounds in notes Squire Allworthy had given Jones—who has flung them from his pockets in grief—must go to London to cash them, presumably to avoid suspicion at a provincial bank. Moreover, he doesn't cash them; like a good capitalist, he asks a banker to invest the money. Unfortunately for George, who finds himself in a novel full of providential chance encounters, Squire Allworthy visits the banker just as George is leaving, and he recognizes the notes. The notion that notes can be *recognized*, yet pass from hand to hand, is of course foreign to us, except in the case of tracing serial numbers. But this is the point: it became increasingly foreign to those who lived in the late eighteenth and early nineteenth centuries, as money slowly became a universal—and therefore impersonal—form of representation. Squire Allworthy perhaps recognized the date on Black George's bills, and certainly the bank of issue. But in the nineteenth century the Bank of England became the only English bank allowed to issue notes, and in 1833 its notes became legal tender. A mere hundred years after *Tom Jones*,

---

[2]Ibid., p. 113. Cf. pages 154–155: Money "comes out of circulation, enters into it again, preserves and multiplies itself within its own circuit, comes back out of it with expanded bulk, and begins the same round afresh." This is exactly the process that occurs in *Colonel Jack*, where pickpocketing comes to represent nascent capitalism. By the end of the novel, the pickpocket Jack has become a merchant dealing in international trade; the final pages read almost like a bill of lading.

Allworthy's notes would have looked like anyone else's. Thus, paper money as we know it was born.

Paper money is nothing if not *fast:* it passes from hand to hand, circulates in society like blood fueled by drink.

The paper money goes about, by one, and two, and five,
A circulation like the blood, that keeps the land alive.[3]

By the first third of the nineteenth century, it has become volatile, expansive, untrustworthy, and eminently transferable. Unlike Colonel Jack, Oliver Twist's pickpocket friends need not rely on rewards for returning purses. Indeed, for them picking pockets has become a business, and the money passes from pocket to pocket as rapidly as today it is wired from coast to coast. Thus, the five-pound note Mr. Brownlow gives Oliver to pay the bookseller is pulled from his pocket by the Dodger, then seized by Fagin, and finally handed over to Sikes, not without reluctance and resentment. Money as a medium of exchange has found precisely the level (pocket high) that will enable it to become the chief social force in people's lives. This impersonal character of money—that it can no longer be recognized—enables it to become a form of representation unlike any other, except perhaps language. " 'I don't see it,' said Lord Lufton. 'I might have a lot of paper money by me, and not know from Adam where I got it' " (Trollope, *The Last Chronicle of Barset*). Paper money is anonymous and mobile, passes from hand to hand without leaving a record, moves like water by seeking its own level, and seems to contain power within itself like a seed. In reality, though, the power is exogenous, a purely social function, a matter of convention. Rooted as it is in the apparatus of mutual compulsion and obligation—in debt—paper money registers like a

[3]Thomas Love Peacock, "A Mood of My Own Mind," *Paper Money Lyrics* (1837), in *The Works of Thomas Love Peacock* (New York: AMS Press, 1967), 7:115.

thin membrane all of society's contrary reactions to debt: shame, horror, giddy excitement. To go into debt is to make a pact with the devil; in Goethe's *Faust* (part 2), paper money is' in fact the work of the devil. With the mushrooming structures of debt and credit in nineteenth-century capitalism, even theft becomes obsolete—or, to say the same thing, becomes a social function like any other. As Frank Greystock says in Trollope's *The Eustace Diamonds*, "To get into a bank at midnight and steal what little there may be in the till, or even an armful of bank-notes, with the probability of a policeman catching you as you creep out of the chimney and through a hole, is clumsy work; but to walk in amidst the smiles and bows of admiring managers and draw out money over the counter by thousands and tens of thousands, which you have never put in and which you can never repay; and which, when all is done, you have only borrowed;—that is a great feat."

Thus we have come full circle. From Defoe's Colonel Jack to Fielding's Black George to Dickens's Oliver Twist, to countless characters in nineteenth-century novels who go into debt—dozens in Trollope alone—money has created its own pockets, great fictional storehouses of representation called banks (or moneylenders) in which all our desires reside. That in the nineteenth century—though the process obviously begins in the eighteenth—novels were also becoming such storehouses is no mere coincidence. Hence the connection between the two topics of this book, which in a sense contain each other: the theme of money in fiction and the nature of literary realism. My assumption is that the account of literary realism is incomplete without an account of other forms of representation, particularly economic ones. But the account of representations, too, is incomplete without an account of the social and material worlds they represent. The realistic novel is an outcome of a complex evolution in the art of representation, an evolution spread stratigraphically across all of human culture—across art, politics, dress, economics, religion. The transition from metal currency to paper money indicates a more general cultural shift that submitted immediate reality to a kind of semantic coding; and the realistic novel was part of this shift. As money was becoming more fictional, fiction was becoming not only more profitable, not merely more concerned with economic themes, but also more mediated, more representational, more omniscient—in a word, more realistic—and consequently less reliant upon the diary, the letter, the memoir, the first person, or the preface that, like so many of Defoe's, claimed the story was literal fact.

One would like to ask someone in the nineteenth century what he or she would consider "real." Would it be land one can walk on, precious metal whose weight and shape and bulk one can feel, or paper—the mere promise to pay such metal? The answer would probably be that the heavier, more substantial things are real. But the nineteenth century found that paper increasingly not only had the power to represent the reality of land and metal but—magically, it seemed--could increase it. Gold and land may have been "real," but paper also became a social force of unprecedented reality. Just so with the novel, which came to represent reality in ways that most people thought of as suspect, new, unstable—even subversive—but that, with a kind of split consciousness, they came to an implicit belief in. The nervous underpinning of this belief was a change in modes of representation, of which money is a key example.

Of course money's function is not merely to represent land or gold. In fact, precisely what it does represent—labor, value, exchange, wealth, commodities, or even (not least) excrement—is a matter of debate (or taste). As we shall see, money is at the very least a sign of reality in the novel, that is, a sign of the rupture of form by reality. But it is also fictional, chimerical, romantic. It dreams for us, as Marx pointed out: "*Money* is the external, universal *means* and *power* (not derived from man as man or from human society as society) to change *representation* into *reality* and reality into *mere representation*. It transforms *real human and natural faculties* into mere abstract representations, i.e., *imperfections* and tormenting chimeras; and on the other hand, it transforms *real imperfections and fancies*, faculties which are really impotent and which exist only in the individual's imagination, into *real faculties and powers.*"[4] In the nineteenth-century novel, money bolsters and fuels the romantic dreams of heroes and heroines from all classes of society at the same time as it discredits those dreams—that is, establishes the limit of their realization. The failure of money, the fact that paper money is money but at the same time the absence of money, parallels in the realistic novel the failure of mimesis, which can never be a pure, homogeneous extension of its world. If the novel represents reality, it does so in ways that acknowledge this failure, that make reality disruptive, that confirm the Real as "that which resists desire."[5] As with money, material reality enacts an inner limit for the novel, one that wells up within it as a kind of subtext.[6]

Behind all this—with roots deep in the sixteenth, seventeenth, and eighteenth centuries—lies the transition from an aristocratic or late feudal society founded on land, rents, and accumulated wealth to a market society founded on capital,

---

[4]Karl Marx, "Economic and Philosophical Manuscripts," trans. T. B. Bottomore, in Erich Fromm, *Marx's Concept of Man* (New York: Frederick Ungar, 1968), p. 167. Italics in the original.

[5]Fredric Jameson, *The Political Unconscious* (Ithaca: Cornell University Press, 1981), p. 184. Cf. Edward Said: "The incorporation of reality into the great realistic novels of the mid-nineteenth century is performed by converting figures of secular authority into forms of sociomaterial resistance faced by the protagonists." *Beginnings* (New York: Basic Books, 1975), p. 95.

[6]Cf. Jameson: "The literary or aesthetic act . . . must draw the Real into its own texture, and ultimate paradoxes are to be traced back to this process, whereby language manages to carry the Real within itself as its own intrinsic or immanent subtext." *Political Unconscious*, p. 81. Compare also John Romano: "The failure of literature faithfully to represent the real is the defining preoccupation of realism. . . . For the novelist's preoccupation with the novel's failure of mimesis inevitably finds expression in the novel's form, which is, then, the form of frustration." *Dickens and Reality* (New York: Columbia University Press, 1978), p. 94.

Introduction

speculation, and a newly aroused hunger for commodities. It is this transition that allows Lionel Trilling to assert that "the novel is born with the appearance of money as a social element."[7] Of course money has always been something of a social element and something of a theme in literature. L. C. Knights's *Drama and Society in the Age of Jonson*, for example, explores the theme of money in Jacobean drama. But in the nineteenth century, first, money has come to replace custom as the major social bond,[8] and second, money itself has evolved into something new and unexpected with the growth of banks and the explosion of credit that preceded and accompanied the Industrial Revolution. Paper money became not only a medium of exchange but an object of imagination and desire—indeed, a "human fiction" and "collective hallucination," according to J. Hillis Miller.[9] In the nineteenth century money became both social glue and social solvent, a leveler and a key to social power, the thing that made people equal and unequal. As Marx wrote, "If *money* is the bond which binds me to *human* life, and society to me, and which links me with nature and man, is it not the bond of all *bonds*? Is it not, therefore also the universal agent of separation [i.e., solvent]? It is the real means of both *separation* and *union*, the galvano-*chemical* power of society."[10] Money instead of custom be-

[7]Lionel Trilling, *The Liberal Imagination* (New York: Doubleday, 1953), p. 203. Cf. Edward Said: "Money is always in evidence during the course of the realistic novel." *Beginnings*, p. 145.

[8]In making this point, Grahame Smith quotes the poet Southey in 1808: "The commercial system has long been undermining the distinctions of rank in society." *Dickens, Money, and Society* (Berkeley: University of California Press, 1968), p. 62.

[9]J. Hillis Miller, afterword to the Signet Classic edition of Dickens's *Our Mutual Friend* (New York, 1964), p. 904. Cf. also Ronald Schleifer in the foreword to *Money Talks: Language and Lucre in American Fiction*, ed. Roy R. Male (Norman: University of Oklahoma Press, 1980), p. x: "Money . . . is a fiction—it is perhaps the great American fiction."

[10]Marx, "Economic and Philosophical Manuscripts," p. 166. Italics in the original.

20

came the chief constraint upon human will; but of course money also spurred will in the form of ambition and self-interest by serving as the universal object of desire.

In the following pages the terms "realism" and "realistic novel" refer more to a time frame than to a limited type, and within them I include novels as different as Jane Austen's *Persuasion* and Knut Hamsun's *Hunger*. In other words, realism is not limited to naturalism, or to whatever it is that, say, Trollope does as opposed to whatever it is that Dickens does. As for method, this is not primarily a historical study, though its ground is history. My assumption is that the novel is both document and form; that the novels that show us attitudes toward money are the same ones that register the effects of those attitudes. So the form takes shape both from its documentary intentions and from the historical pressures of the world it documents. There are risks, of course, in approaching novels as historical documents; the novel is not simply a window upon history.[11] But neither is it purely a set of tropes and rhetorical strategies. In many respects this book is a new rhetoric of fiction, but the term *semantic* would be more accurate: a semantic of fiction, because the meaning of realistic fiction is always social, its strategies are never purely formal, and its signs are political as well as aesthetic.

Marxists are right in pointing out that often (they would say always) the aesthetic is a product of the political and form is a product of history. But this doesn't mean that money in its various manifestations, especially paper, "caused" or "deter-

---

[11]But compare Engels, who said that in Balzac he found a "complete history of French society from which, even in economic details (for instance, the rearrangement of real and personal property after the Revolution) I have learned more than from all the professed historians, economists, and statisticians of the period together." Cited in Fredric Jameson, *Marxism and Form: Twentieth Century Dialectical Theories of Literature* (Princeton: Princeton University Press, 1971), pp. 10–11.

mined" realistic fiction; rather, both are results of a historical process, and both in turn modify that process. Money in this book stands for both larger economic forces—the Industrial Revolution in particular—and "smaller" psychological ones: desire, need, ambition. Like the novel, it functions metonymically, though like the novel it is also a form of representation whose properties demand scrutiny in themselves. Did the Industrial Revolution "cause" the widespread use of paper money or vice versa? Does desire give rise to money or money to desire? The futility of searching for univocal causes should be obvious. The richness of the term "money" stems from its power as a mediator: between the individual and history, between the aesthetic and the economic, between the social and the material. Money offers itself as the most convenient of a number of keys to open up the world of the nineteenth-century novel and let us understand that world as it slides into our own. I deal not so much with causes or determinations as with a reciprocity of effect, a mutual qualification of history and form (or art or culture or thought) as both unfold.

And in this respect I am not a Marxist. I don't believe that social and economic reality always determines thought or that understanding modes of production is the single most important key to history. But I do accept much of the Marxist critique of capitalism, especially as it applies to the nineteenth century. One cannot understand the realistic novel and its precipitate slide into modernism without Marx and his followers; they are in many respects the best guides. And I am especially sympathetic to Fredric Jameson's description of the way dialectical criticism transcends "that sterile and static opposition between formalism and a sociological or historical use of literature between which we have so often been asked to choose."[12] Jameson has been an inspiration for this book, as have a number of other Marxist and neo-Marxist thinkers:

[12]Ibid., p. 331.

Marc Shell, Edward Said, Georg Lukács, and Walter Benjamin. Of these, Benjamin's example is the most congenial for my purposes, particularly the Benjamin of *Illuminations*, the Marxist whose ideology is subsumed under the forms of the polite essay and metaphoric thinking: the Marxist as phenomenologist as aphorist. My own point of view, in fact, owes more to phenomenological thought than to Marxism. But if phenomenological thought is to survive Derrida it must change, and in my case the change consists of a greater emphasis upon dialectical thinking, upon the dynamic interplay of presence and absence.

My method, then, is heterogeneous, and my language is as much metaphoric and literary as it is theoretical, if only because in my view theory should always be sullied by the concreteness of events. Theory should free us to investigate reality rather than provide us with a set of immutable conclusions. But theory and metaphor have this in common: both clamp forceps on the truth and may damage it in the process. In this respect, even so noted a theoretician as Marx was a metaphoric thinker. I tend to agree with Kurt Heinzelman's suggestion that *Capital* is one of the great three-decker nineteenth-century novels, complete with plot and characters (Mr. Moneybags, the simple laborer, Free-Trader Vulgaris), at least in part 2.[13] And to call it a novel is not to show it any disrespect or to lessen its truth value—only to assert that its truth, like a novel's, is provisional, elusive, and contingent: an investigation of reality.

As a phenomenologist, I aim to elucidate in all its complexity the "world" of realistic fiction: its unique fix upon the material and social worlds and its characteristic ways of unfolding in time. But none of this would be possible without an understanding of the historical and economic realities that re-

[13]Kurt Heinzelman, *The Economics of the Imagination* (Amherst: University of Massachusetts Press, 1980), pp. 181–182.

verberate through the realistic novel. *Reverberate:* "If a written sentence does not reverberate at every level of man and society, then it makes no sense" (Sartre).[14]

I make no attempt to be exhaustive, to trace every reference to money in the realistic novel. My examples are intended to be representative, and in the absence of any other principle of selection, I dwell upon those novels I've judged to be worth our time, those that dramatize most powerfully their own inner limits, their enactment of social and physical reality. A subsidiary aim has been to open the canon to include novels such as *Persuasion* or *Hunger* or *The Gambler* as well as the more familiar examples of the period. At the same time, the mass of material upon which this book is grounded has compelled me at times to stand at a middle distance in order to see it all and to make connections, and such a position has obvious dangers. To resist reducing novels to mere illustrations, then, the sustained readings become more sustained as the book proceeds, and I beg the reader's indulgence if at the beginning the camera seems to pan too quickly or too incessantly.

All this said, let us put aside considerations of theory or method for the matter at hand: a voyage through a world connected with ours, but distant enough in time to require a guide. This book began as a labor of love, but under a corrective impulse. For a number of years I have been dissatisfied with my treatment of the realistic novel in my first book, *The Garden and the Map.* I have no intention of criticizing—as I did in that book—a genre or literary period because of the ways culture or history shines through it. It isn't difficult to detect the hum of the factory beneath, say, the sentences of Henry James, but this doesn't diminish him as a writer. Quite the contrary: it makes him better. It may be difficult for some to accept the paradox that great works of art could be produced in an age of commodity hunger, love of money, and imperi-

---

[14]Quoted in Jameson, *Marxism and Form,* p. 201.

alism of the kind J. Hillis Miller describes in the opening chapter of *Poets of Reality*—a voracious ego hunger to dominate and even devour the physical world and its inhabitants, the not-I. Actually, the age of the realistic novel was more divided against itself than such a list of its horrors, genuine though they were, would suggest. In Balzac, Dickens, Eliot, Melville, Flaubert, Dostoevsky, and James, as well as in their lesser contemporaries, we repeatedly see the giddy excitement of an unstable social and economic world of booms and busts,[15] of speculative bubbles swelling and bursting, of the gambling mentality—the sense of life out on a limb or about to soar or crash—as well as the disgust all this shades into and becomes mired in.

Fiction writers are generally a subversive lot anyway, not merely because the novel was born out of satire and parody, and not only because the realist in particular labors under the negative obligation to refrain from idealizing reality, but perhaps primarily because in the realistic novel the social character of behavior is everywhere embedded in the lives of individuals—in their morals, their scruples, their fortunes, their clothes, their airs, their disillusionments, their failures, their marriages. As we shall see, this social character comes to be inscribed in the very form of the novel—in the semantics of realistic fiction—as well. In the nineteenth century the results are that astonishing collection of novels whose power to undermine their own most cherished assumptions is still undiminished: *Persuasion*, *La Cousine Bette*, *Great Expectations*, *The Confidence Man*, *Our Mutual Friend*, *Little Dorrit*, *Middlemarch*,

---

[15]The nineteenth-century monetary crises in England: 1824–1825, 1837, 1839, 1847, 1857, 1866, 1873. See Brian Murphy, *A History of the British Economy* (London: Longman, 1973), pp. 510–511, 612–618. The narrator of Butler's *The Way of All Flesh* mentions the 1846–1847 crisis several times as a turning point in his life. In the preface to *Little Dorrit*, Dickens acknowledges basing the financial crash in that novel upon this same crisis.

Introduction

Madame Bovary, Hunger, The Wings of the Dove, The Brothers Karamazov, The Gambler, The Mayor of Casterbridge, and many more—architectural wonders constructed on quicksand, which is precisely their wonder.

CHAPTER ONE

Misers and Spendthrifts

Though they weren't necessarily listening to each other, when it came to money nineteenth-century novelists could speak with one voice. "Money is life. Money is all powerful," says Balzac's Père Goriot. The narrator of Dostoevsky's *The Gambler* exclaims, "Money is everything!" In Dickens's *Our Mutual Friend* Bella says, "I have money always in my thoughts and desires," and in Hardy's *The Return of the Native* Diggory Venn echoes her: "Money is all my dream." Dr. Thorne, in Trollope's *Doctor Thorne:* "A rich man can buy anything." Dombey, in Dickens's *Dombey and Son:* "Money, Paul, can do anything."

Bromfield Corey's statement in *The Rise of Silas Lapham* may serve for the entire century: "But there's no doubt but money is to the fore now. It is the romance, the poetry, of our age. It's the thing that chiefly strikes the imagination."

Such comments could be multiplied, and they will be in the course of this and the following chapters. But the question naturally occurs: Couldn't similar remarks be ferreted out of other centuries as well? For example, an eleventh-century Frenchman, cited by Fernand Braudel: "Money, not Caesar, is everything now."[1] Or Francis Bacon in the early seven-

---

[1] Fernand Braudel, *The Structures of Everyday Life: The Limits of the Possible,* vol. 1 of *Civilization and Capitalism, 15th–18th Century,* trans. Miriam Kochan and Siân Reynolds (New York: Harper and Row, 1981), p. 511.

teenth century: "No man can be ignorant of the idolatry that is generally committed in these degenerate times to money, as if it could do all things public and private."[2] Is the nineteenth century unique, then? Or do we tend to see the worship of money in any period we look at closely, much like J. H. Hexter's description of the historian who sees the rise of the middle class as typical of the period he specializes in?[3]

There are several answers to this question, none of them simple. We might begin by pointing out that from approximately the fifteenth to the nineteenth century the middle class in Europe was steadily and continuously on the rise, so that historians who isolate one century or a portion of a century and note the bulge are in a sense correct; but they are noting a fragment of a continuous curve. The same could be said with regard to money, though there are qualitative differences too in the eighteenth and nineteenth centuries. Braudel sees capitalism as a phenomenon "gradually gaining ground" in Europe from 1400 to 1800.[4] Naturally the love of money would gain ground in this period too, though the consciousness of the idolatry of such love, of course, goes back to Paul's First Epistle to Timothy—and before. In a sense the nineteenth century was the climax to a movement whose slow beginnings reach back to antiquity. The nineteenth century

[2]Cited in L. C. Knights, *Drama and Society in the Age of Jonson* (New York: George W. Stewart, n.d.), p. 123.

[3]See Fernand Braudel, *The Wheels of Commerce*, vol. 2 of *Civilization and Capitalism*, *15th–18th Century*, trans. Siân Reynolds (New York: Harper and Row, 1982), p. 479.

[4]Fernand Braudel, *Capitalism and Material Life*, *1400–1800*, trans. Miriam Kochan (New York: Harper and Row, 1973), p. xiii. Braudel's *Civilisation matérielle et capitalisme* was first published in France in 1967 and later was revised extensively by the author. The book cited here is the English translation of vol. 1 of the unrevised *Civilisation matérielle et capitalisme; The Structures of Everyday Life* and *The Wheels of Commerce* are the new English translations of volumes 1 and 2 of Braudel's revision (vol. 3 is forthcoming). I am quoting here some comments in the preface to *Capitalism and Material Life* that were dropped in *The Structures of Everyday Life.*

was also "a violent breakthrough, revolution, total upheaval,"[5] as Braudel says—but one whose preparation was long in the making. As Braudel shows in his massive three-volume study, the Industrial Revolution was not the beginning of capitalism, but the final climactic stage of a long process in which its characteristic devices and apparatus—credit, speculation, bills of exchange, banks, investment capital—evolved largely out of international trade. "With the coming of steam," he says, "the pace of the West increased as if by magic. But the magic can be explained: it had been prepared and made possible in advance. To paraphrase a historian (Pierre Léon), first came evolution (a slow rise) and then revolution (an acceleration): two connected movements."[6]

This increased pace of life in the late eighteenth and early nineteenth centuries was something palpably felt, and it certainly contributed to that sense of an economy and society heating up and rushing about, of which money became a chief image. (The other chief image, at least in the second half of the nineteenth century, was the railroad.) For by the nineteenth century money was qualitatively different from money in previous ages: it was symbolic money—paper. Again, the roots of this change go back several hundred years, and it was still in progress in the nineteenth century. The widespread *acceptance* of paper money, however, is unique to the nineteenth century and is one of the major reasons such universals as "everything" and "anything" so often surface in remarks about money. Money was "the thing that chiefly strikes the imagination" because its power to a great extent resided *in* the imagination, in contemplating its power. Of course, its possession entailed unexpected difficulties: once gained, it could be lost, and consequently much of one's energy had to be expended not in exercising that wonderful power, but in turning it to the end of preserving and increasing itself. Particularly in the form of

[5]Ibid., p. x.
[6]Braudel, *Structures of Everyday Life*, p. 372.

paper, it could easily be lost—as novels like Dickens's *Little Dorrit* and Trollope's *The Way We Live Now* dramatize—so the acceptance of paper money was always qualified by lingering distrust, as we shall see. Dickens and Trollope describe the typical nightmare of speculation: the (largely dishonest) business venture that draws in hordes of investors and turns out to be a bubble. But such nightmares would not be possible without the dream of sudden fortune also made possible by paper money and speculation. In the nineteenth century money came to the fore in part because people had learned what large amounts of it could do, in the form of capital, and because paper money came to symbolize this volatile, expansive force of capital. Paper money is a "circulation like the blood"[7] because without it all that energy would dissipate. It "keeps the land alive"[8] because it touches everyone, rich and poor, and enmeshes society from top to bottom in a common set of values, most of which boil down to the importance of obtaining money.

None of this happened overnight, however. The history of paper money is the history of an ancient institution greeted with distrust by almost everyone except merchants and traders. As Braudel points out, China had paper money as early as the ninth century, though it disappeared by the fourteenth, and Islam had developed most known forms of paper money by the time of the Crusades.[9] In the West—in Europe and England—the "discovery" of paper money in the late seventeenth century was a rediscovery: "As soon as men learnt to write and had coins to handle, they had replaced cash with written documents, notes, promises and orders."[10] But such men were almost exclusively merchants. Others used

---

[7] Thomas Love Peacock, *Paper Money Lyrics*, in *The Works of Thomas Love Peacock* (New York: AMS Press, 1967), p. 115.
[8] Ibid.
[9] Braudel, *Structures of Everyday Life*, pp. 452 and 472.
[10] Ibid., pp. 471–472.

metal—gold, silver, and copper coins—or paid each other in kind (in produce or commodities), or bartered. In England paper money developed very slowly in the seventeenth century and scarcely was used outside London.[11] Its two chief forms were the goldsmith's note and the bill of exchange. In London and Stockholm in the late seventeenth century, goldsmiths discovered they could retain just a percentage of their depositors' gold in the till and lend out the rest at interest. The receipt or note the goldsmith (or banker) gave his depositor was a promise to pay him cash, but it came to be "passed from hand to hand as a substitute for cash."[12] Even more common a substitute were bills of exchange (bills issued against a consignment of commodities), which merchants often sold to lenders at a discount. According to Braudel, bills of exchange became so widely used in most European countries that by the eighteenth century the sheer volume of paper money—especially bills of exchange—exceeded that of hard currency.[13] I should emphasize again, however, that this was a specialized money, still used almost exclusively by merchants and traders. "'I propose,' said Mr. Micawber, 'Bills—a convenience to the mercantile world, for which, I believe, we are originally indebted to the Jews, who appear to me to have had a devilish deal too much to do with them ever since—because they are negotiable.'" Micawber is wrong about the Jews—the West

[11]L. A. Clarkson, *The Pre-Industrial Economy in England, 1500–1750* (London: B. T. Batsford, 1974), p. 146.

[12]Charles Wilson, *England's Apprenticeship: 1603–1763* (London: Longman, 1965), p. 208. In addition to the works cited, I have also relied for factual matters in the following pages upon several other books: by J. H. Clapham, *The Bank of England: A History*, 2 vols. (Cambridge: University Press, 1970); *An Economic History of Modern Britain*, vol. 1, *The Early Railway Age* (Cambridge: University Press, 1950); and *The Economic Development of France and Germany, 1815–1914* (Cambridge: University Press, 1968). Also, Brian Murphy, *A History of the British Economy* (London: Longman, 1973), and P. G. M. Dickson, *The Financial Revolution in England: A Study in the Development of Public Credit, 1688–1756* (London: Macmillan, 1967).

[13]Braudel, *Wheels of Commerce*, p. 113.

learned the practice of issuing bills of exchange from Islam[14]—but otherwise correct: merchants used them, banks and money brokers cashed them, and like bank notes they were negotiable and came to be passed from hand to hand as a substitute for coins, the only currency previously in use. Thus the notes Defoe's Colonel Jack steals from a gentleman's pocket are both goldsmith's notes and bills of exchange.

But the very specialized nature of such forms of paper marks them as distinct from most paper money in the nineteenth century. By the nineteenth century, even workers were often paid in bank notes, especially in England.[15] "From 1797 to 1821," says Robin M. Reeve, "gold coins virtually disappeared from circulation: instead the country relied upon bank notes, about half of which were Bank of England notes while the remainder were issued by country banks."[16] In 1833, Bank of England notes became legal tender; after 1844 no new banks could issue notes, and bank notes other than those issued by the Bank of England gradually disappeared. Money, like capital, became impersonal and mobile. One followed upon the other, and both developments were inseparable from the Industrial Revolution. Of course, as Braudel repeatedly points out, the habit of lending capital for industry (especially mining) and for trade was firmly established before the Industrial Revolution.[17] But in 1760, says T. S. Ashton, "there was nothing that could justly be called a capital market. Lending was still largely a local and personal matter. By 1830 the volume of investable funds had grown beyond measure. Banks, and other institutions, served as pools from which capital, brought by innumerable streams, flowed to industries at home and abroad. . . . Capital was becoming impersonal—

[14]Braudel, *Structures of Everyday Life*, p. 472.
[15]Robin M. Reeve, *The Industrial Revolution, 1750–1850* (London: University of London Press, 1971), p. 170.
[16]Ibid., p. 168.
[17]Braudel, *Wheels of Commerce*, pp. 321–325 and 385–395.

'blind,' as some say—and highly mobile."[18] Statistics bear this out and underline the nineteenth century's special claim to be the age of money; for example, the increase of banks in England from 280 in 1793 to 626 in 1815.[19]

All this said, it is important to keep in mind that old habits of thought persisted, especially as a refuge against the new. The nineteenth century is characterized not so much by the conquest of paper money as by the long-drawn-out transition, extending back to the previous century, from older forms of wealth to paper. Many still thought of gold as the only real money and land as the only stable and secure form of wealth. We shall look at land in detail in the following chapter; for now I want to concentrate on the psychology of a period in which *both* gold and paper are the things "that chiefly strike the imagination." In the pages that follow I use "gold" in a metonymic sense, to stand for all metal currencies—gold, silver, copper—of which gold was always the most valued.

In the first place, gold and silver coins were commodities as well as a medium of exchange. They were traded, hoarded, and melted down, as Braudel points out.[20] But they were money too, symbolic and material at the same time. As Michel Foucault puts it, money in the sixteenth century not only represented wealth, it was itself wealth.[21] Such a view was still available to the nineteenth century, if chiefly as nostalgia. One who felt threatened by the instability of a society whose middle ranks were swelling, in which wealthy merchants with marriageable daughters were knocking on the doors of the impoverished aristocracy, might well feel inclined to regard gold as the only real form of wealth. Gold conformed to Locke's definition of money: "Some lasting thing that men

[18]T. S. Ashton, *The Industrial Revolution, 1760–1830* (Oxford: Oxford University Press, 1970), p. 87.
[19]Reeve, *Industrial Revolution*, p. 167.
[20]Braudel, *Wheels of Commerce*, pp. 194–204.
[21]Michel Foucault, *The Order of Things: An Archaeology of the Human Sciences* (New York: Pantheon Books, 1970), p. 169.

33

might keep without spoiling."[22] The grammatical ambiguity here is telling: money is the way *we* keep from spoiling, the way we defer death indefinitely. In a well-known scene in *Dombey and Son* Paul asks his father, "Papa! what's money?" To the answer that money can do anything, Paul counters with the obvious question: "Why didn't money save me my mamma?" Dombey—who by now wants to escape this conversation and perhaps review his assets—acknowledges that money cannot save people whose time has come to die, but very often *can* keep death off for a long time altogether. Even this crumb of comfort, though, is belied by Paul's subsequent death. Indeed, it is this very scene that makes his father suspect the boy is sickly and needs special care.

Though Dombey is not exactly a miser, he is someone who hoards, who keeps things close, who refuses to spend any sympathy on his surviving child, Florence. In fact he exudes such gloom in the novel precisely because he shares the miser's closed personality without availing himself of the miser's source of comfort: poring over his piles of wealth. For misers these piles of wealth are invariably coins, usually gold. We cannot imagine a miser hoarding bills and notes; what he hoards must not perish, because it keeps him alive. Those attracted to paper are speculators and profligates. Gold is material, palpable, valuable in itself, whereas paper is an abstraction, a fiction. The point is that *both* gold and paper were social forces in the nineteenth century; they may have been ships passing, but the passage was slow. Indeed, for most of the century they were linked; England's money was on a gold standard, largely because of the earlier examples on the Continent of floating currencies that turned out to be (in Defoe's term) chimerical: John Law's Mississippi Company notes, and the assignats issued after the 1789 revolution. In France, too, the Bank of France, created in 1800, issued notes convertible to gold and silver, though paper money took longer to catch on

[22]John Locke, *Of Civil Government* (New York: Dutton, 1924), p. 140.

in France than in England.[23] Thus Balzac's novels are filled with details of bills being signed, passed back and forth, renewed, discounted, and dishonored; but when Rastignac sends for his sisters' money in *Le Père Goriot*, it arrives as two sacks of gold. In other words, it comes from the provinces, where paper is more suspect than in the city.

Transporting gold in such a manner seems almost anomalous—and clearly is done in *Le Père Goriot* only because of Rastignac's desperation—because gold tends to stay in one place, in contrast to paper, which is inclined to circulate. Gold is hoarded, paper spent, gold is stable and paper unstable, gold attracts misers and paper spendthrifts. In the nineteenth century the miser is still a recognizable literary type, but his portrayal tends to shade into that of the rich merchants and businessmen (like Dombey) who love money and business and nothing else. The attraction of money for the businessman is similar to that of gold for the miser: it insulates against change and decay, is susceptible to tidy manipulation, and centers, even immobilizes, one's life. "His money was never naughty; his money never made noise or litter, and did not spill things on the table at meal times" (Butler, *The Way of All Flesh*). The businessman in novels usually shares the miser's anal-retentive character, though perhaps with less manifest satisfaction.

Behind Dickens's financiers, behind the Dombeys, Merdles, and Podsnaps, lurks the shadow of the miser, who often is presented as a relic of previous centuries, like Fagin in *Oliver Twist*. The nineteenth-century miser, like his literary progenitors, is always old, often babbling, sometimes bordering on second childhood. Sir Pitt Crawley in *Vanity Fair*, Peter Featherstone in *Middlemarch*, Scrooge in *A Christmas Carol*, Silas Marner, old Grandet in *Eugénie Grandet*, old Séchard in *Illusions perdues*, Gobseck in Balzac's "M. Gobseck," Rigou in *Les paysans*—their nostalgia for a past in which the representation of wealth and its material reality were one usually spills

---

[23]Braudel, *Structures of Everyday Life*, p. 474.

over into a kind of arrested infancy. Boffin, the fake miser in
Our Mutual Friend, is also a kind of literary miser, and he
learns about being a miser (while pretending to have his appetite for it whetted) by paying Wegg to read to him about
famous misers of the past. In *Silas Marner*, George Eliot presents the standard picture of the miser, transparent enough in
our post-Freudian age: "How the guineas shone as they came
pouring out of the dark leather mouths! . . . He spread them
out in heaps and bathed his hands in them; then he counted
them and set them up in regular piles, and felt their rounded
outline between his thumb and fingers, and thought fondly of
the guineas that were only half-earned by the work in his
loom, as if they had been unborn children."[24] The miser is
usually a misanthrope because he cannot live in the present.
He longs for the time when a hoard was a hoard, when things,
and their value, never changed. *Never changed* means not only
that they didn't decrease—the usual justification for a
hoard— but that they didn't increase either, as was generally
the case in the expanding economy of the nineteenth century.
It was this expanding economy and all it represented—
change, increase, the unknown, the future—that the nineteenth-century miser deliberately drew back from, longing for
a (supposed) earlier and simpler world. For the miser money is
time, and time piles up; time is what he hoards and stores,
walling himself in against the future. All his desire pours into

[24]Compare this with the description of Trina in Norris's *McTeague:* "Trina would play with this money by the hour, piling it and repiling it, or
gathering it all into one heap and drawing back to the farthest corner of the
room to note the effect, her head on one side. . . . Or, again, she would
draw the heap lovingly toward her and bury her face in it, delighted at the
smell of it and the feel of the smooth, cool metal on her cheeks. She even put
the small gold pieces in her mouth and jingled them there." In Freud's
scheme, excrement is aliment. These descriptions of misers find their grotesque culmination in a passage in Beckett's *Malone Dies:* "Yes, a little creature, I shall try and make a little creature, to hold in my arms, a little
creature in my image, no matter what I say. And seeing what a poor thing I
have made, or how like myself, I shall eat it."

his hoard in order to harden and kill desire, so he can become, in George Eliot's phrase, "a mere pulsation of desire." Silas Marner's coins are monads, solid and weighty: the essence of material reality, primitive, inert, and immutable. Paper money, on the other hand, is weightless and flighty—it has wings, cannot stay put. The opposite of the miser is the spendthrift, a literary type for the most part new to the nineteenth century. Mr. Sowerby in Trollope's *Framley Parsonage*, George Vavasor in *Can You Forgive Her?* Felix Carbury in *The Way We Live Now*, Maxime de Trailles in several of Balzac's novels and stories, the Baron Hulot in *La Cousine Bette*, Rosamond Lydgate in *Middlemarch*, Dmitri Karamazov in *The Brothers Karamazov*, Alexis in *The Gambler*, Becky and Rawdon Crawley in *Vanity Fair*—all these characters thrive out on a limb, in a world of their own fiction, spending money they don't even possess ("Borrowing is the best way of sustaining credit," says Rastignac in Balzac's *La peau de chagrin*). In the nineteenth century, paper money represented an explosion of money that took on the quality of a collective fantasy. Around the edges of that explosion, the spendthrift became a kind of holy fool; in *The Brothers Karamazov*, everyone trails behind and gathers around Dmitri as he tosses his money about. Like Dmitri, most spendthrifts are compulsive and asocial. They create an artificial conviviality by buying social energy and companionship. Often they are outcasts or misfits because they fail to understand or have turned away from the traditional male role of earning or managing money. In fact, the spendthrift in the nineteenth-century novel is often a woman—Madame Bovary, Rosamond Lydgate, Becky Crawley—for whom money isn't real. And they are right. It isn't. Money for the spendthrift is the paper image of money. As Defoe says, "Substance is answered by the Shadow. . . . the Name of the thing is made Equivalent to the Thing itself."[25]

[25]Daniel Defoe, *The Chimera: or, The French Way of Paying National Debts Laid Open* (London: T. Warner, 1720), p. 6. This book was written by Defoe

On the other hand, paper money possesses the reality of power. It has, if nothing else, exchange value. It can't store value, like gold; its status is the very opposite of the chest of gold and silver coins Robinson Crusoe finds on the wreck and drags to his island, even though he can't spend it. The impotence of Crusoe's money is a little allegory of nascent capitalism in the early eighteenth century, just before banks and credit began to expand. Once that expansion was under way, the power of paper money swelled. We sense it expanding toward the future, swelling credit, swelling capital. This does not happen for the miser, whose desires contract, whose world shrinks. But it happens for the spendthrift, who flees the past and devours the future, who spends money in order not to have it, in order to continuously desire it. The spendthrift spends as quickly as possible to hasten the moment when he has nothing and the future takes on the character of the unknown. One doesn't become a spendthrift by having a store of money to spend. The spendthrift perpetually empties the store before it can become a store. Somehow there's always more to spend. He borrows, gambles, marries into money. His compulsive generosity is really no more generous than a miser's sense of security is secure. Only Balzac could detect an element of calculation in such compulsion. In *La peau de chagrin*, he has Rastignac say, "When a man spends his time squandering his fortune, he's very often onto a good thing: he is investing his capital in friends, pleasures, protectors and acquaintances. . . . If he has the bad luck to lose his capital, he has the good luck to be appointed tax collector, make a good marriage, become the secretary to a minister or an ambassador. He still has friends and reputation, and is never short of money."[26] The last statement is true of all spend-

---

in response to John Law's experiment with paper money in France (the Mississippi Company), apparently just before the bubble burst.

[26]The translation of *La peau de chagrin*, *The Wild Ass's Skin*, is by Herbert J. Hunt (Harmondsworth: Penguin Books, 1977).

thrifts: they are never short of money. Only the miser is short of money. A few notes, a few coins are plenty for the spendthrift—they are no more real than a fortune. The only reality is the lack of money. The more money the spendthrift has, the more he spends, and the less he has. Alexis, in Dostoevsky's *The Gambler*, spends two hundred thousand francs in three weeks. This kind of spending can happen only with paper. Gold possesses a gravitational pull that prevents it from being tossed around. But gold is always there in the background for the spendthrift, defining by contrast the weightlessness of paper.

Indeed, in a certain respect the miser and the spendthrift are two sides of the same coin. They are linked by a historical necessity imperfectly expressed by Gresham's law, that bad money drives out good: in the nineteenth century this meant that gold was hoarded and paper spent. Maxime de Trailles says to the miser and moneylender Gobseck (in Balzac's story "M. Gobseck"), "if there were no spendthrifts, what would become of you? The pair of us are like soul and body." The spendthrift Maxime deals primarily with paper—countless notes, some signed by several hands, that he discounts to obtain cash. And Gobseck deals primarily with gold; he distrusts paper, using it only as a means to get his hands on more gold. For both of them, money is not only money but the lack of money. This reciprocal play of money and its lack is contained within money, within its dual nature, and therefore embedded in nineteenth-century society.

Behind all this is a changing conception of the nature of wealth. Misers and spendthrifts are grotesques, parodies of an older and a newer conception of wealth. Etymologically, wealth comes from weal, or well-being. Before the eighteenth century and especially the nineteenth—and surviving in the latter as nostalgia—wealth was thought of as a store of value representing stability and security. In England, as we shall see, its most powerful symbol was not gold, but the landed estate. As Trollope put it in *The Last Chronicle of Barset*, "land is about the only thing that can't fly away." But with the Industrial Revolution and the financial revolution that helped make it possible, wealth gradually came to be thought of as something different, as an active agent, a power. This new sense of wealth meant that money was not only a medium of exchange, but a means of expansion and increase, of augmentation, amplification, multiplication. It became a way to extend one's sphere of influence over nature and society, fuel for the newly discovered voracious ego—which in fact it gave birth to. Especially in the form of paper money, wealth became volatile, unpredictable, patulous. Defoe saw this aspect of money as "meer Air and Shadow, realizing Fancies and Imaginations, Visions and Apparitions,"[27] as indeed it was at times, particularly in the kinds of bubbles Dickens and Trollope portray in *Little Dorrit* and *The Way We Live Now* and to a lesser degree Butler displays in *The Way of All Flesh*.

For this reason, in *Little Dorrit* the irony of Mr. Dorrit's inheriting an estate lies in the context created by the more volatile states of wealth surrounding him—not only Merdle's financial schemes, but also the business debts that have caused Dorrit to spend so much of his life in debtor's prison. The estate is the nineteenth century's link with the past, but for Mr. Dorrit it arrives in the form of a treasure discovered under a rock, of manna from heaven (though of course it turns out to be a curse rather than a blessing). Dickens's juxtaposition of the factors that impoverished and enriched Mr. Dorrit—his business debts and later his inheritance—demonstrates the degree to which by the mid-nineteenth century the domain of the gentry and nobility (landed estates) was being invaded by the middle classes. It also suggests that this analysis of social types has confined itself so far to only one class of society. To complete the picture—to make clear exactly what the older notion of wealth entailed—it now becomes necessary to con-

[27]Defoe, *Chimera*, pp. 5–6.

sider not the dialectic of gold and paper, but the wider one of land and money. And for that we turn first to Trollope and then to Jane Austen.

CHAPTER TWO

The Breaking up of
the Estate: *Persuasion*

The obligation to maintain an estate—to improve it or at the very least keep it whole for one's heirs—prevented most country squires in nineteenth-century England from becoming either misers or spendthrifts. The miser was a throwback to an older, perhaps more primitive bourgeois world, the spendthrift the product of a newer urban one. The sons of squires, however, and particularly the sons of neighboring lords—usually the second or third son, with no estate or title to inherit—often do appear in eighteenth- and nineteenth-century novels as notorious profligates (owing to habits they have learned at Oxford or Cambridge, of course). They are images of the landowner's chief fear, that the need to raise cash will drive him to mortgage or sell part of his estate. Since feudal times, estates had generated money through rent rolls. But by the eighteenth century rents were not enough to pay for the increasingly expensive entertainments of the landed gentry and nobility, entertainments such as gambling, visiting, the season in town, and the Grand Tour, which were signs of their station as gentlemen.[1] Land, of course, was

---

[1]See Charles Wilson, *England's Apprenticeship: 1603–1763* (London: Longman, 1965), pp. 256–260. Wilson adds to this list the eighteenth-century

financially secure—"the safest investment for a man seeking to maintain the value of his capital" and "the best security for borrowing money."[2] Thus, those with land found themselves in the unique position of creating their insecurity out of their very security. If the owner of an estate borrowed on his land, he could lose the land; but if he did not, he might lack the money to cover his expenses. By the last quarter of the nineteenth century Trollope could see very accurately where all this had led:

> In the year 1800 the Carbury property was sufficient for the Carbury house. Since that time the Carbury property has considerably increased in value, and the rents have been raised. Even the acreage has been extended by the enclosure of commons. But the income is no longer comfortably adequate to the wants of an English gentleman's household. If a moderate estate in land be left to a man now, there arises the question whether he is not damaged unless an income also be left to him wherewith to keep up the estate. Land is a luxury, and of all luxuries is the most costly. (*The Way We Live Now*)

In Trollope we see two recurring figures who are the products of this situation: the embarrassed squire or lord in debt, and

---

mania for building lavish country mansions. It should be noted also that rents gradually decreased as England shifted from an agricultural to an industrial base. The proportions of this shift are astonishing: in 1688, 80 percent of the labor force was in agriculture; by 1901 this figure was 8.5 percent. See "The Growth of National Incomes," by W. A. Cole, in *The Cambridge Economic History of Europe*, vol. 6, *The Industrial Revolutions and After*, ed. H. J. Habakkuk and M. Postan (Cambridge: University Press, 1965), p. 45.

In general terms, all this is true of the Continent as well; for example, Braudel points out that expenditures of the landed gentry in eighteenth-century France were steadily rising. Fernand Braudel, *The Wheels of Commerce*, vol. 2 of *Civilization and Capitalism, 15th–18th Century*, trans. Siân Reynolds (New York: Harper and Row, 1982), p. 260.

[2]Wilson, *England's Apprenticeship*, pp. 258 and 257.

the impoverished gentleman (often the son of the former) who must marry for money. Both are present in *The Way We Live Now*, his great late novel, and in the early *Doctor Thorne*, the most popular of all his works during his lifetime. Before we turn to Jane Austen, it may be helpful to look at Trollope, who often makes explicit matters that she is content to hint at. His first novel appeared only twenty-nine years after her last, but at times the two writers appear to inhabit vastly different yet obviously homologous worlds. The genuine dialectic of land and money that generates much of the tension in Austen's novels becomes in Trollope a mock battle, a ritual, because in fact money has already won, though land is still there (with its jewels, those splendid estates), defining by contrast the world that has been lost, the world whose values have become decorative. Trollope defines the terms that lie embedded in Austen so that we can perhaps see them more clearly; in fact he points them out explicitly, with less subtlety and with obsessive repetition—a kind of vulgar Jane Austen. Austen's world was perched on the brink of a slide into money; Trollope's was already there. Behind all this we should be able to sense the accuracy of Marx's comment in *The Eighteenth Brumaire:* "But in the course of the nineteenth century the urban usurer takes the place of the feudal lords, the mortgage the place of the feudal obligation attached to the land, and *bourgeois* capital the place of the aristocratic estate."[3]

The values associated with land in Trollope are the opposite of those associated with money—security and stability rather than greed, satisfaction rather than desire—but repeatedly his landed gentry are forced to cash in the former for the latter. In *Doctor Thorne*, Squire Gresham is so deeply in debt that the only hope for preserving his estate lies in urging his son to marry an heiress. As Trollope points out in a later novel (*The Way We Live Now*), marrying heiresses "has become an institu-

[3]Cited in Georg Lukács, *Studies in European Realism* (New York: Grosset and Dunlap, 1964), p. 35.

tion, like primogeniture, and is almost as serviceable for maintaining the proper order of things. Rank squanders money; trade makes it;—and then trade purchases rank by re-gilding its splendour." The necessity of marrying for money is one of Trollope's most obsessively recurring themes, though in this he was typical of the century. The complication in *Doctor Thorne* is typical too: Frank Gresham is in love with someone poor—in fact, Mary Thorne is also a bastard—and resists his family's pressure to marry the various heiresses they hunt up for him, though all comes out right in the end in this massive, three-volume fairy tale, when the bastard miraculously turns out to be—what else?—an heiress. The difference between this fairy tale and Jane Austen's social comedies is that Austen was more aware of the hypocrisies involved, whereas Trollope succumbed—in this instance, at least—to wish fulfillment. Money in *Doctor Thorne* attains the level Trollope obviously wished it to attain, rising from the lowborn (the Scatcherds) through the agency of Mary, the hybrid democrat-heiress, the bastard of good blood—the mediator between low and high— back up to where it belongs in the best of all possible worlds, in the hands of the gentry. We shall see the figure of the mediator again in Jane Austen, in the character of Anne Elliot in *Persuasion*. In *Doctor Thorne* Trollope makes his heroine a bastard (an outsider) in order to display two value systems converging in her, but in this case the mediator figure is so schematic that Trollope fails (unlike Austen) to see its implications. Mary has democratic sympathies, but she believes in inheritance even before she becomes an heiress. Democracy of course is presumed to be blind to privilege, and so is money. Yet this novel would have us believe that the best-born naturally deserve to possess, have a right to possess, and in the past always *have* possessed, money. Furthermore, if they don't possess it now, they must marry to attain it—they must even marry beneath them, thus invalidating their claim to status. Fortunately for the gentry, women have less of a claim to status than men, whose names and titles they assume, so that

Frank Gresham *can* marry a bastard when she turns out to have inherited a fortune, even if she does believe in democracy, that is, in the priority of worth or merit over status.[4] In all of this we can see that money was the Trojan horse by means of which the upper classes introduced democracy into a world they were also—with money—desperately attempting to fortify against democracy.

But none of these questions are resolved, or even sufficiently dramatized, in *Doctor Thorne*. The almost incestuous course of money in the novel—a debt is satisfied by marriage of the debtor's heir to the creditor's heiress—demonstrates the degree to which Trollope wanted his world to be insular, closed. He could often write wisely of money, but in this novel he prefers English gardens. The ending is a true squirmer, with its happy marriage, its hypocrites (such as the De Courcys) let off the hook, its family feuds settled, its enemies welcoming and receiving each other. A duke kisses a bastard!—because now she has money. Trollope proves himself to be the ultimate hypocrite, though, when, after rewarding love with money, he says that "love can only be paid in its own coin: it knows no other legal tender."

Of course, as we shall see in Jane Austen, it is practically impossible not to be to some degree hypocritical when social codes are in conflict. I have begun with *Doctor Thorne* not merely to prove Austen's superiority (that should be obvious) but to demonstrate that the difference between the two writers can be seen in *Persuasion*, whose plot bears some similarity to that of *Doctor Thorne*. In *Persuasion*, the heroine is persuaded by her father not to marry a man beneath her in "circum-

---

[4]Toward the end of the novel, Lady Amelia's letter to Augusta Gresham points out that a gentleman of rank may marry beneath him and pull the woman up, so to speak; but for a woman to marry beneath her is to be pulled down. Of course Trollope is satirizing this strict codification of manners too; later on, Lady Amelia not only marries beneath her, a lawyer, but marries the very person she is advising Augusta in this letter to refuse.

stances" (that is, money), but both daughter and father agree to the marriage eight and a half years later, after the father's circumstances have been reduced by debt and the young man's raised by war, in which he has made a fortune. There is hypocrisy in this too—the reward for steadfast love is not only marriage, but money—but, as we shall see, Jane Austen inscribes it into the text itself in strange, compelling ways.

Trollope, on the other hand, so longed for a world in which land and all it represented could exist in an unfallen state that in *Doctor Thorne* he took extreme (and transparent) measures to restore it. He willed his characters back into Paradise. Of course in other novels he could be more realistic. Mr. Sowerby in *Framley Parsonage*, for example, loses Chaldicotes, his estate, to the Duke of Omnium, to whom it is mortgaged. At his best, Trollope could be a faithful recorder of social change in his time, as the following three passages may reveal. The first, from *Framley Parsonage*, illustrates the conventional attitude toward land, tinged by those survival instincts that impel one to grip more tightly the thing one is in danger of losing:

> "Never let the estate decrease in your hands [Lady Lufton tells her son]. It is only by such resolutions as that that English noblemen and English gentlemen can preserve their country. I cannot bear to see property changing hands."
>
> "Well, I suppose it's a good thing to have land in the market sometimes, so that millionaires may know what to do with their money."
>
> "God forbid that yours should be there!" And the widow made a little mental prayer that her son's acres might be protected from the millionaires and other Philistines.
>
> "Why, yes: I don't exactly want to see a Jew tailor investing his earnings at Lufton," said the Lord.[5]

[5] Lady Lufton's attitude has its roots deep in English society. In the seventeenth century Sir John Strode said: "As oft as thou sellest a foot of

The reference to the Jew tailor is typical of Trollope's insular world, which, because of its need for money, is threatened by outsiders. But what else are the outsiders in England (whose definition depends on the definer) to do with their money when they want to make it secure? Centrifugal money changes hands, but centripetal land stays put, which is the reason some of those with money want to buy it. This quandary is typical of the age. Wealthy tradesmen grow old and want to secure their wealth for their families; they want to transform volatile money into stable land and to avail themselves of the privileges of land—"position and influence and political power, to say nothing about the game" (Archdeacon Grantley in *The Last Chronicle of Barset*.)[6] In *Tom Jones*, the Nightingale brothers both had made money in trade, but while one went on to become a banker, the other "purchased a small estate . . . and retired into the country." In *Faust*, part 2, the fool in the paper money scene turns out to be wise (the text suggests) when he uses his paper money, of which he is instinctively suspicious, to purchase an estate. Similarly, the Bingleys in *Pride and Prejudice*, having made money in trade, are looking for an estate to purchase, and Heathcliff in *Wuthering Heights*, whose "mysterious fortune marks him as a protocapitalist,"[7] returns to establish the life of a country squire.

But this very convertibility of money into land, which Lady

---

land, thou disposeth of a furlong of thy credit"; and in the eighteenth century—prefiguring the conflict Trollope describes—Henry Bolingbroke said, "The landed men are the true owners of our political vessel, the moneyd men as such, are no more than passengers in it." Strode is quoted in Lawrence Stone, *The Crisis of the Aristocracy* (London: Oxford University Press, 1967), p. 75, and Bolingbroke in P. G. M. Dickson, *The Financial Revolution in England: A Study in the Development of Public Credit, 1688–1756* (London: Macmillan, 1967), p. 28.

[6]Compare Fernand Braudel: "Land did not instantly confer titles of nobility, but it was a step in the right direction, a means of social promotion." *Wheels of Commerce*, 249.

[7]Fredric Jameson, *The Political Unconscious* (Ithaca: Cornell University Press, 1981), p. 128.

Lufton rightly fears, demonstrates that land can never be as stable, insular, centripetal, and secure as it once was. Whether it ever actually possessed these qualities in some distant feudal past is irrelevant; from the point of view of a time when the invading bourgeoisie can purchase land and set themselves up as gentry, the previous age is seen as a veritable garden, in which land was primary and money merely one of its attributes. Lady Lufton conjures up the chastising mirage of this age in her insistence that land should never change hands; but the buried metaphor she employs undermines the insistence. Already land is thought of in terms of the medium that passes from hand to hand; it is merely another object for sale, with its price tag, like shoes or carriages. Land has become an attribute of money.

Thus the convertibility of money and land, once it becomes a common social possibility, can move in both directions. In *Middlemarch*, Peter Featherstone wills his land to his natural son, who immediately sells it to the local banker and sets himself up as a money changer. Trollope's most evil character, George Vavasor, cannot wait to sell the estate he will inherit from his grandfather. And as we shall see, Mr. Elliot's only interest in inheriting Kellynch Hall in *Persuasion* lies in having the auctioneers sell it.

The other two passages from Trollope illustrate the implications of this convertibility. The first, from *The Last Chronicle of Barset*, is part of a conversation between Johnny Eames and Miss Madalina Demolines (who speaks first):

> "But don't you feel now, really, that City money is always very chancy? It comes and goes so quick."
> "As regards the going, I think that's the same with all money," said Johnny.
> "Not with land, or the funds. Mamma has every shilling laid out in a first-class mortgage on land at four per cent. That does make one feel so secure! The land can't run away."
> "But you think poor Broughton's money may?"
> "It's all speculation, you know."

"The funds" often mentioned in English novels of the eighteenth and nineteenth centuries are the funded national debt. "City money" means money created or made or invested in London's financial district, within the original boundaries of the city. Trollope no doubt intended this passage to be read as a mild satire upon the rising middle class. Like the speculator Dobbs Broughton, Miss Demolines possesses money but not status, even though she refers to her (or her mother's) wealth in terms of status, that is, land. But it is not land she owns, it is mortgaged land—land her mother holds the mortgage on. She may feel secure, but her money marks her as just as déclassé as the Mr. Broughton she looks down upon, with his City money. The satire is directed toward a middle class with its own fine distinctions of rank and status, which amount to no more than the distinctions between safe and chancy money—the high bourgeoisie and the bourgeoisie mired in finance. And the presence of land in the midst of this scale is part of the satire: it is merely another investment.

In a similar passage (the final example), Lady Eustace, whose title itself is a joke, clasps a necklace around Miss Macnulty's throat in *The Eustace Diamonds* and asks, "How do you feel, Julia, with an estate upon your neck? Five hundred acres at twenty pounds an acre. Let us call it five hundred pounds a year." Here the rapid conversions from jewelry to money to land to money (that is, rent) demonstrate that land is merely another commodity and that it too is to be measured by money, whose value is calculable in precise terms, though, as her cousin points out, Lady Eustace's figures are wrong. The calculations are not as important, however, as the act of the imagination in performing them. The estate around Miss Macnulty's neck has dissolved the jewels for a moment, but *all* dissolves, the most solid things, in the imagination of money.

We might term this theme, with Georg Lukács, the breaking up of the estate. In his essay on Balzac's *Les paysans*, Lukács shows that this process—far more advanced in France than in England because of the revolution—gave rise to a class of bourgeois financiers who made a killing by lending money to peasants interested in purchasing small pieces of partitioned estates.[8] One senses everywhere in the French novel of the nineteenth century this absorption of land by money. Julien Sorel's ambition for greatness in *Le rouge et le noir* is flawed because (without noble blood) he fails to conceive of it as financial greatness, an oversight novelists later in the century would correct. Still, surrounding Julien constantly is the "foul atmosphere of petty financial interests,"[9] especially in the provinces. In *Le rouge et le noir*, the provinces equal money, but Paris equals disdain of money, at least by those who can afford to disdain it. With this bifurcation, land as a value becomes lost in between. "I'm going to seek solitude and rustic peace," says Saint-Geraud (whose story Julien overhears on the coach to Paris), "in the only place they exist in France: in a fifth-floor apartment overlooking the Champs-Elysées." Thus, he has put his chateau at Monfleury up for sale, after enduring for four years the horrors of the provinces, which have been overrun by the inferior classes.

It would be easy to make too much of this difference between the French and the English and to see in Stendhal's contemporary, Jane Austen, a charming throwback to a more bucolic existence in which the provinces are still a garden untrodden by coarse boots. Certainly, Austen's vision is selective. As Raymond Williams says, "What she sees across the land is a network of propertied houses and families, and through this tightly drawn mesh most actual people are simply not seen."[10] Though there is nothing in Austen to equal that startling opening of *Le rouge et le noir*, with its noise of the nail factory, Williams's statement nonetheless is not entirely

---

[8]"Balzac: The Peasants," in Lukács, *Studies in European Realism*.

[9]The translation of *Le rouge et le noir*, *The Red and the Black*, is by Lowell Bair (New York: Bantam Books, 1958).

[10]Raymond Williams, *The English Novel from Dickens to Lawrence* (New York: Oxford University Press, 1970), p. 24.

true. In *Persuasion*, with the eruption of contingency represented by Louisa's fall, we suddenly see—of all things—working people: "By this time the report of the accident had spread among the workmen and boatmen about the Cobb, and many were collected near them, to be useful if wanted; at any rate, to enjoy the sight of a dead young lady, nay, two dead young ladies, for it proved twice as fine as the first report." Such marvelous wickedness coming at a moment of great emotional turmoil in the novel cannot be accounted for by the portrait of Jane Austen as an Emily Dickinson, as a lively spirit living a subdued and insular existence—a portrait just as false for Dickinson as for Austen. Jane Austen's seismograph was every bit as sensitive as Balzac's or Stendhal's (and more so than Trollope's). In her we see the first substantial rumblings of the fall from land into money, the first cracks in the plaster. And in *Persuasion* we see all the dizzying implications of this fall; indeed, the novel is disrupted by a series of literal falls that prove as crippling to the text as to the world of English country estates.

The manifest themes of *Persuasion* are typical of Jane Austen: prudence versus love, persuasion versus fixity of purpose, woman's versus man's faithfulness (which branches out to include the differing estates of women and men). The story of love diverted, deflected, misunderstood, but eventually regained and the resolution (marriage) are also typical. But *Persuasion* is about none of these things. Of all Austen's novels, it is the one that most invites us to read through (or misread) its apparent intentions. In the first place, by comparison with her others the novel is clipped, abbreviated. Of course she was ill while writing it, already dying of Addison's disease. One senses that she may have grown tired of her old strategies and that her chief interest now lay in subverting them—not by irony (as many, led by Mark Schorer, have asserted about her earlier work), but by the accumulated weight of seemingly peripheral matters, of subplots and minor characters, and the accompanying shrinkage, even disappearance (until the obligatory marriage), of her main character, Anne, her most self-effacing heroine since Fanny in *Mansfield Park*.

The novel begins when Anne's father, Sir Walter Elliot, finds himself forced to rent out Kellynch Hall because he is embarrassed by debt. To this point in Jane Austen's novels money has certainly been a factor, but not money in its various volatile states, not debt or speculation or sudden losses or gains of money. Neither have there been the extremes of character made possible for subsequent novelists by money: no spendthrifts (though some firstborn sons are injudicious), no misers (though a few characters are tightfisted), no profligates driven to distraction by debt, no thieves, speculators, or families made suddenly wealthy by a lucky inheritance. It is true that some of this is present as though at the edge of Austen's world; Margaret in *Sense and Sensibility* says, "I wish that somebody would give us all a large fortune apiece!" and Miss Crawford in *Mansfield Park* plays the card game Speculation with reckless abandon ("No cold prudence for me"). But Margaret's wish isn't granted (as it is, say, in *Great Expectations, Little Dorrit, The Portrait of a Lady,* or *The Wings of the Dove*), and Speculation remains a card game. For the most part, money in Jane Austen is what it has been for centuries, a medium of exchange, not capital. Edmund Bertram in *Mansfield Park* is forced to be content "only not to be poor" because he is a gentleman—therefore work and trade are out of the question—and a second-born son—therefore no inheritance. His only option is to enter the clergy and obtain a living. In Edmund's world, money is passed through families, inherited, tied to estates, and any other means of obtaining it except through a living—itself tied to land—is out of the question. Again, however, there are hints of a different world. Mary Crawford tells Edmund, "Be honest and poor, by all means— but I shall not envy you; I do not think that I shall even respect you. I have a much greater respect for those that are honest and rich." But until *Persuasion* these are only hints.

In *Persuasion*, Sir Walter has mortgaged his estate but still cannot afford to pay his debts, and now must rent it and find someplace else to live. He is even referred to at one point as a spendthrift, though his character is too subdued by vanity and the obligation to appear respectable to remind us of those wild, manic spendthrifts in Balzac and Dostoevsky. Still, the fall from land into money is clear, and Austen doesn't dwell on its horrors, simply because she regards them as self-evident. But the precedence of land in her world may be verified by a look at several other novels. In *Pride and Prejudice* the distinction between the Bingleys and Mr. Darcy is in a sense a distinction between money and land. "I am astonished," Miss Bingley says, "that my father should have left so small a collection of books. What a delightful library you have at Pemberley, Mr. Darcy!" His reply: "It ought to be good; it has been the work of many generations." In other words, money buys books, but only taste and good judgment, which are "the work of many generations" because they are tied to the stability of a place, a landed estate, can build libraries. Miss Bingley then turns to her brother, and this exchange follows:

"Charles, when you build *your* house, I wish it may be half as delightful as Pemberley."

"I wish it may."

"But I would really advise you to make your purchase in that neighborhood, and take Pemberley for a kind of model. There is not a finer county in England than Derbyshire."

"With all my heart; I will buy Pemberley itself if Darcy will sell it."

"I am talking of possibilities, Charles."

"Upon my word, Caroline, I should think it more possible to get Pemberley by purchase than by imitation."

Bingley is no fool (unlike his sister), and the point of his compliment is, of course, that neither is possible; if Pemberley could be purchased it could be imitated too, for both courses

54

flow from the power of money. But if Pemberley could be purchased it would not be Pemberley, and everyone in the room knows that.

In Jane Austen's world the chief characteristic of land is that it cannot be purchased. Land *already* exists. It spreads its continuity into the past and (presumably) into the future as well. Money, by contrast, comes to the fore as an object of desire and imagination. In *Sense and Sensibility*, when Marianne imagines that just enough money (a "competence") will buy her "a proper establishment of servants, a carriage, perhaps two, and hunters," she is of course imagining the right sort of marriage, but in an embryonic way she is contemplating the power of money, and in the very act she has ensured that such a world is lost to her—it has become an object of desire. The repeated lesson of nineteenth-century fiction (its clearest formulation is in *Great Expectations*) is foreseen here by Austen: that money will buy anything except what money has come to supplant, well-being.

Thus, land in Jane Austen has something of the flavor of a recent unfallen state that can be regained only through marriage. Marianne wants to imagine a "competence" because in fact her mother and sisters have been dispossessed of their estate. Ideally, marriage should have always already occurred, like being born into a "proper establishment," but then Austen would have nothing to write about. Her heroines must get married for the same reason that they have been dispossessed: because they are women. Though land is always prior in Austen, its title can never be possessed by her women, who must marry to enjoy its advantages. Thus they are forced to desire in order not to desire. "It is only the lot of those who are not obliged to follow any [profession], who can live in a regular way, in the country, choosing their own hours, following their own pursuits, and living on their own property, without the torment of trying for more; it is only *their* lot, I say, to hold the blessings of health and a good appearance to the utmost." This is said at the end of a long speech in *Persuasion* about the disadvantages of the various professions, made by Mrs. Clay, a widow herself engaged in one of the two professions open to women in nineteenth-century England: seeking to become married. The irony here is that the object of her intentions, Sir Walter, is embarrassed by debt, but she doesn't give up until she discovers (beyond the boundaries of the text, of course) that other profession for which only Jane Austen could find a term of consummate politeness: at the novel's end she is said to be living in London under the younger Mr. Elliot's "protection."

The key phrase in Mrs. Clay's statement is "without the torment of trying for more." Land, like marriage, means release from desire. So marriage *into* land contains a double guarantee of that release. Money on the other hand means enslavement to desire, to the necessity of always needing or wanting more, a necessity Sir Walter has lately been prey to. But land means release from necessity. In a sense, novels cannot be written in a world where land is the sole reality and something like money doesn't exist (only poems and masques can), because novels unfold through desire and necessity. Novels cannot be set in Paradise. In this one respect, *Persuasion* is similar to Austen's other novels, most of which enact a fall from Paradise.[11] As we've seen, *Sense and Sensibility* opens when Mrs. Dashwood and her daughters are forced to move from Norland Park because the late Mr. Dashwood's son by a previous marriage has inherited it. Similarly in *Pride and Prejudice*, the fall at least threatens, since Mr. Bennet's property is entailed "in default of heirs male, on a distant relation." In *Mansfield Park*, in a variation of this theme, the heroine is dispossessed of her parents and home and brought to live in a "proper establishment," though initially at least this is felt as a fall. Only *Emma* begins without such a fall, though Jane Aus-

---

[11]Alistair Duckworth points out that *Mansfield Park* contains an expulsion from the Garden scene. *The Improvement of the Estate: A Study of Jane Austen's Novels* (Baltimore: Johns Hopkins University Press, 1971), p. 25.

ten finds an ingenious way to suggest the regaining of Paradise at the novel's end: the marriage of Emma and Mr. Knightly restores Donwell Abbey to its original wholeness, because Hartfield was "a sort of notch" in Donwell. When a heroine in Austen is expelled from the Garden, she is also decentered. She no longer occupies the nucleus of her existence, unlike, say, Mr. Woodhouse in *Emma*, who "from his fortune, his house, and his daughter . . . could command the visits of his own little circle." Repeatedly, the words "circle" and "center" appear in the novels. "Their estate was large, and their residence was at Norland Park, in the centre of their property" (*Sense and Sensibility*). "Their homes were so distant, and the circles in which they moved so distinct . . ." (*Mansfield Park*). "Marrying early and having a very numerous Family, their movements had been long limited to one small circle" (*Sanditon*, her unfinished novel). All these circles are made to be broken, but the one in *Persuasion* is ruptured several times over: by the loss of Anne's mother, the loss of Captain Wentworth, and finally the loss of Kellynch Hall. Of those decentered in Austen's novels, Anne thus seems the blankest, the one most emptied. In talking with the Musgroves, she learns "another lesson, in the art of knowing our own nothingness beyond our own circle." This is a conventional Austen observation, but applied to Anne it seems curious, since up to this point in the novel—her visit to Uppercross—she has clearly been shown to be someone who in fact is nothing *within* her own circle.[12] She possesses an elegant mind and a sweet disposition (a generic heroine), but she "was nobody with either father or sister; her word had no weight, her convenience was always to give away—she was only Anne." *Her word had no weight.* Repeatedly, Anne's reluctance or inability

---

[12] Tony Tanner also makes this point in his recent essay, "In Between— Anne Elliot Marries a Sailor and Charlotte Heywood Goes to the Seaside," in *Jane Austen in a Social Context*, ed. David Monaghan (Totowa, N.J.: Barnes and Noble, 1981), p. 187.

to speak is mentioned. "How eloquent could Anne have been!" "Anne longed for the power of representing to them all what they were about." "Anne said what was proper." For the first two-thirds of the novel, her responses in conversation are more often than not summarized instead of presented, and we cannot resist feeling that this represents Jane Austen's own devaluation of her heroine; that is, she treats Anne as those in her family do, who "had no inclination to listen to her." Indeed, Anne treats herself this way: "Anne's object was not to be in the way of anybody."

Of course, the presumed intention of all this is to demonstrate that what appears to be weakness and timidity is really strength, as evidenced by the steadfastness of Anne's love over eight and a half years. But the theme is a tired one and is undercut by too many other considerations. The first sign of Anne's weakness had occurred before the novel began when she caved in to her father's and Lady Russell's persuasion not to marry Captain Wentworth. Their compelling argument is that Captain Wentworth lacks means—that is, either money or property—a lack that by the novel's end has been rectified. One senses that by then Anne's strength is all in retrospect. In fact, it is she who now lacks means, her family's income having been reduced by debt. Love conquers all, but in this case love can afford to; Captain Wentworth now possesses a fortune of twenty-five thousand pounds. "Captain Wentworth, with five-and-twenty thousand pounds, and as high in his profession as merit and activity could place him, was no longer nobody. He was now esteemed quite worthy to address the daughter of a foolish, spendthrift baronet, who had not had principle or sense to maintain himself in the situation in which Providence had placed him, and who could give his daughter at present but a small part of the share of ten thousand pounds which must be hers hereafter." Sir Walter is of course an easy and deserving target, but Anne is by no means an innocent bystander in all this. Indeed, she comes to exist in the novel at the intersection of conflicting social codes by means of which true value (or love) sheds or dons the protective covering of financial considerations according to the situation.

Thus her initial choice—to accept or reject Wentworth—represents a double bind. To accept him would be to ignore the social code by which a nineteen-year-old is expected to respect the advice of her elders. It would also be to accept reduced circumstances. To reject him, however, is to equate that social code with financial survival, to accept the linkage of moral worth and money. The source of the problem, then, is the social code itself, which is ambiguous, in flux. As Raymond Williams says, Jane Austen's world "is indeed that most difficult world to describe, in English social history: an acquisitive high bourgeois society at the point of its most evident interlocking with an agrarian capitalism that is itself mediated by inherited titles and by the making of family names." Thus, "an openly acquisitive society, which is concerned also with the *transmission* of wealth, is trying to judge itself by an inherited code and the morality of improvement."[13] Anne's blankness as a character—indeed, her near invisibility to some of the other characters—may be due to her functioning as a mediator between these conflicting codes. Austen gives her the nearly impossible task of reconciling the morality of self-sacrifice with that of self-interest. She may even be termed (in Max Weber's phrase) a "vanishing mediator,"[14] one whose purpose in the novel is to form a bridge not merely between changing social codes but between all the intolerable antinomies of her world: the vanity of her father and the love of Captain Wentworth, the good manners of the Captain and the false ones of Mr. Elliot (or the boorish ones of her family), the only slightly tarnished respectability of her name and the sheer poverty—the nothingness—of Mrs. Smith's ("a mere Mrs. Smith, an every-day Mrs. Smith, of all people and all names in the world," rants her father), the lofty world of

[13]Williams, *English Novel from Dickens to Lawrence*, p. 21.
[14]See Jameson, *Political Unconscious*, p. 279.

marriage and the sordid one of debt and dishonor, the feudal world of the titled nobility and the bourgeois one of economic security[15] (her father's baronetcy is itself a kind of mediating title between the nobility and gentry). The impossibility of forming such links and at the same time becoming a "character" as we usually understand that term in fiction is demonstrated by her strange emptiness, her sense of being hollowed out. She is a vanishing mediator because she enables a new kind of character, a new type, to come into existence, one whose status will always be crippled by economic considerations (as so many characters in this novel are literally crippled). Thus she marries Wentworth, and the novel proves to be (like all of Austen's) a social comedy—but the evil Mr. Elliot will still inherit Kellynch Hall and may very well still "bring it with best advantage to the hammer," as he had intended when younger. In other words, the marriage restores no Paradise; unlike her sister, "Anne had no Uppercross Hall before her, no landed estate, no headship of a family."

As a mediator, Anne occupies the center of the novel, the intersection of its various characters. She is the only one whose inner life is visible to us, and thus the only one we cannot see right through. But to the others she is repeatedly a substitute, someone who must care for her nephew so her sister can go to dinner at the big house, someone indeed who nurses others throughout the novel. At Uppercross she is literally the social medium, the go-between, "treated with too much confidence by all parties, and being too much in the secrets of the complaints of each house." The others speak *through* her. "She could do little more than listen patiently, soften every grievance, and excuse each to the other." For the

[15]Cf. Tony Tanner: "Anne Elliot is no longer of the old nor yet does she belong to the new. She does not disapprove of the Musgrove children but 'she would not have given up her own more elegant and cultivated mind for all their enjoyments.' Nor can she find self-realization in her father's house. She is in between." *Jane Austen in a Social Context*, p. 181.

reader she possesses a dense inner life—in fact, Jane Austen may insist too much upon her feelings, in the absence of anything else to insist upon—but for her fellow characters she is patronized, ignored, used, talked through. She acts as umpire, sounding board, servant, nurse. One senses that for Anne to act for herself would be to send out ripples entirely unreciprocated by the world, to find herself with a shoreless existence. Of course, this isn't entirely true. She does act for herself by approaching Captain Wentworth at the concert, but we sense in this that Captain Wentworth is precisely the device she requires to enable her to fold back upon herself, to become substantial. There is, incidently, one other mediator in the novel who serves both as a parody of Anne and as a warning: Mrs. Smith's Nurse Rooke, who tells her mistress the secrets of Bath society, from which the crippled Mrs. Smith in her squalid quarters is excluded. Like Anne, Nurse Rooke (who never actually appears in the novel) nurses others, listens to their complaints, and passes along their secrets, but unlike Anne—except by association—she has more than a touch of slime to her, as is clear from her function as a gossip, a disseminator of salacious information, and from her name, more characteristic of Dickens than Austen. Furthermore, through the agency of Nurse Rooke, at Bath Anne is still the repository of secrets (including the central one of the novel, regarding Mr. Elliot), a function whose importance for the development of the realistic novel I will discuss in chapter 4. (Cousine Bette in Balzac's novel of that title serves the same purpose, as we shall see, though her character is hardly sweet like Anne's.) Nurse Rooke and Mrs. Smith are in a sense disruptions in this narrative, reminders of the thin ice Anne Elliot treads. Anne may not herself be sordid, but she is far from being untouched by sordid things—they threaten her at every step.

Indeed, the threatening presence of the sordid in this novel—sordid because of economic associations—is what is new for Jane Austen. We shall see it again in Henry James. It is as though a trapdoor has revealed for an instant the cloacal cellar beneath a fine country house. The novel is interrupted by a series of falls, or near falls, which of course are not interruptions but part of its strategy. Still, they *function* as interruptions, as eruptions of contingency in the normal, seemingly timeless flow of events in English country life. Sir Walter's metaphoric fall is the first, the fall that echoes Austen's continuing preoccupation with the fall from Paradise. But there are also the literal falls of young Charles Musgrove and of Louisa, the former resulting in a dislocated collarbone, the latter in a severe concussion. Furthermore, the Admiral and Mrs. Crofts, Captain Wentworth says, often take spills in their carriage. And Anne herself, reeling from the emotions of Captain Wentworth's second proposal, appears to Mrs. Musgrove to have fallen. It takes the latter some time to assure herself "that there had been no fall in the case; that Anne had not at any time lately slipped down, and got a blow on her head; that she was perfectly convinced of having had no fall." Of course, Anne *has* fallen—in love—another kind of disruption with its own barely suggested sordid associations. We sense in all these falls, both metaphoric and literal, a fall of the human body from grace. Someone who falls finds that her body has become a weapon turned against her. The earth rears up, solid and unredeemed. The world becomes known as a material world. The same when one's body is crippled; one becomes immobile, often supine, more subject to gravity. Cripples abound in this novel as well: Captain Harville is lame and Mrs. Smith crippled. Louisa's mobility is reduced by her fall, as though she were crippled too; "there is no running or jumping about, no laughing or dancing."

Mrs. Smith is the text's most sedentary cripple, though— one who never moves, a kind of immobile secret herself at the heart of the novel. Her secret of course is financial disaster, much more severe than that experienced by Sir Walter, and her crippled state is obviously allegorical. In this little allegory we see, however, another conflation of the moral and financial in *Persuasion*; as a youth, she had "lived for enjoyment," suggesting that her downfall is perhaps deserved. "We were a thoughtless, gay set, without any strict rules of conduct." It is at least clear that if a base existence did not result in her fall, her fall resulted in a base existence. Of course Mr. Elliot materially contributed to it too, by leading her husband into ruinous expenses, expenses that, if they resembled his own, were "disposed to every gratification of pleasure and vanity." Mr. Elliot's conduct flows from a social code obviously appalling to Anne, a code unattached to history and one whose chief motivation is self-interest. "I have often heard him declare," says Mrs. Smith, "that if baronetcies were saleable, anybody should have his for fifty pounds, arms and motto, name and livery included." Yet Mr. Elliot's conduct makes a telling comment upon that of Anne, for whom social codes are in conflict. Anne may very well marry Captain Wentworth for love, but her conscience is surely eased by the money he now conveniently possesses. To assert, as Alistair Duckworth does about Jane Austen, that "it is a consistent mark of moral integrity in her novels that solely financial considerations be excluded from personal decisions"[16] may be stretching a point, particularly with regard to *Persuasion*.

One way of understanding all this may be to say that Mr. Elliot's conduct—echoed in Mrs. Smith's and Sir Walter's and faintly echoed in Anne's—is not conduct at all, in the way Jane Austen would understand the word. "Conduct" implies

[16]Duckworth, *Improvement of the Estate*, p. 30. Duckworth's book dismisses the notion of Schorer and others (going back to D. W. Harding) that Austen subverts the apparent values of her novels with scathing irony. Duckworth's emphasis upon the symbol of the estate in Jane Austen is laudable, but the title of this chapter demonstrates my judgment of his wrong emphasis in regard to *Persuasion*, whose "new directions" he thinks may be granted "too much prominence" (p. 26). The issue is not whether Austen is subversive—in *Persuasion* this is clearly the case—but what form the subversion takes. The linguistic ironies of Schorer? It goes further than that. The presence of money and its sordid associations becomes in *Persuasion* a subversive subtext, disrupting the narrative and prefiguring a new kind of novel to follow upon Jane Austen's heels.

guidance, self-regulation. Conduct is behavior conscious of its past and future, of its antecedents and consequences. Mr. Elliot, however, behaves without regard to consequences, and we sense in Mrs. Smith's report of him the suggestion that he simply *acts*, perhaps for immediate gratification, a suggestion whose moral horror for Austen would approach that raised by Ivan Karamazov when he says that everything is lawful. But this is precisely the horror buried in *Persuasion*—that the solution to conflicting social codes is no code at all, but pure contingency. With no code, all acts become accidents, and novels are no longer possible. When Louisa falls, "she was too precipitate by half a second" in jumping down into Captain Wentworth's arms, and although this obviously begins as an act, it becomes an accident, an act displaced from the past and the future, a dislocated act.

For all its deliberateness, Mr. Elliot's plan to sell Kellynch Hall suggests the same threat of contingency as Louisa's accident. "My first visit to Kellynch," he says in the letter Mrs. Smith reveals to Anne, "will be with a surveyor, to tell me how to bring it with best advantage to the hammer." The hammer here is the auctioneer's hammer: Mr. Elliot will divide and sell the estate, which is thus for him merely a commodity. But the hammer also conjures up images of a more brutal division, of the reduction of all that an estate represents—tranquillity, security, the conservation of the past—to mere raw material, to wood, stone, and dirt. Mr. Elliot's hammer threatens to knock Kellynch Hall from the feudal world into the world of high capitalism: out of society—at least society as Jane Austen knew it—into the world of matter.

CHAPTER THREE

The Revenge of
the Material

When members of a culture slip easily into the perspective that enables them to recognize that land and great houses, whatever else they may be, are also dirt and wood and stone, literary realism becomes possible. Realism occurs when the social world undergoes a gradual erosion by the material, a process historically set in motion by the Industrial Revolution and the forms of money that accompanied it. In this chapter and the next I shall attempt to approach a definition of literary realism, first by way of the image of money in novels—and, through that image, of physical objects—then by way of the figure of the eavesdropper and voyeur, who creates the sharp division between self and world out of which realism grows.

Money is one of the most recurring signs of reality in fiction. As a sign of reality, it takes on an ambivalent physical existence. On the one hand, it is an object among other objects and thus has a material status; in the case of Dickens's dust heaps and "paper currency" (the trash blown down London streets) in *Our Mutual Friend*, or of Mr. Cheesacre's piles of manure (which are money to him) in Trollope's *Can You Forgive Her?* or of the misers' piles of gold in *Silas Marner*, *Eugénie Grandet*, and *McTeague*, money becomes the image of a kind of

65

prime matter or raw material, the world reduced to lumps and heaps of denuded objects and waste.

On the other hand, money is an abstraction, a social power, and even (or especially) a sign of the appearances and illusions novelists are fond of stripping from their characters. As we shall see, this is more true of Balzac than of almost any other novelist. In Balzac, appearances are always peeling back like wallpaper to reveal the crumbling plaster beneath.

This schizophrenia of money expresses moral attitudes—money is sordid, money gives us wings—and lends itself in particular to novels of social mobility, in which the contrast between the low and the high is crucial. Behind it lies a sense of material reality implicit in the West's binary habits of thought: matter's nature is to *exclude*, and it excludes everything that is not matter—space, the abstract, the immaterial—in order to become what it is. Attitudes like this go all the way back to the Greek atomists (by way of Newton and Descartes)[1] but receive a new emphasis with that massive social and economic change in the late eighteenth and early nineteenth centuries known as the Industrial Revolution. The Industrial Revolution confirmed a growing sense in the West that the physical world consisted of largely inert raw material to be shaped into commodities by human industry. Commodities by definition have price tags. In a customary society, some objects are more valued than others not because of their price, but because of their relation to the past or to various members of the social order, such as the king or clergy. But there can be no hierarchy among objects once they all have price tags, except of course the purely quantitative hierarchy of money. Objects were bought and sold long before the nineteenth century, of course; but more than ever, goods previously made by hand and used by the maker (cloth especially)

[1]See my *The Garden and the Map: Schizophrenia in Twentieth Century Literature and Culture* (Urbana: University of Illinois Press, 1973), especially chapter 1.

were now made by machine and sold for cash. The story has been told frequently and is familiar: in the eighteenth and nineteenth centuries the West underwent a dramatic shift from a largely handicraft culture with local markets to a society in which even, or especially, the lowest classes paid with wages for what they consumed, instead of making it themselves, bartering for it, being paid in kind, or all three.

And changes in forms of money expressed this shift. With the growth of paper money, money of account—the notional units of measurement in a currency, such as the pound, the livre, or the sou—became that much more an abstract system of quantification, a means of weighing and measuring the value of commodities. Behind paper money, defined by virtue of its absence, metal currency became reduced to the state of leftover matter. Consequently we see in novels (Balzac is the best example) that objects, clothing, houses, furniture, and flesh all take on a common physical status, all are pieces or fragments of leftover matter, signs of a partial and quantified world. As money becomes more symbolic, reality becomes more reductively material, and in this way a truly physical world first enters literature, a world whose physical existence is actually quite threatening. The sense that Sartre's character Roquentin has in *La nausée* that the world is de trop begins with nineteenth-century realism, especially with Sartre's countrymen Balzac, Flaubert, and Zola. In the realistic novel all objects have price tags, without which they are worthless matter, and conversely money itself is worthless matter with value attached to it by a social contract. In its unstable worthless/valuable state, money is like the dust heaps that produce a fortune in *Our Mutual Friend,* or like the cheap paper made from vegetable pulp in Balzac's *Illusions perdues* that has the potential to earn millions.

With the Industrial Revolution money takes on its own autonomy and power, and so do objects. They are no longer part of a continuum of human existence, a means absorbed into human life. The means has become an end. Dickens's most powerful image of this is Venus's shop in *Our Mutual Friend*, half-dark and cluttered with human parts for sale: hands, eyeballs, legs, skeletons, skulls, fetuses in jars. (The image of the dismembered body part also occurs in later novels dealing with money: McTeague's huge gilded tooth in *McTeague*, or Doctor T. J. Eckleburg's eyes in *The Great Gatsby*. In both cases the body and its parts have become objects, commodities.) The experience of money, especially as gold gives way to paper, is the experience of a desire for a certain end transforming itself into the desire for the means by which all material ends are satisfied. In this way desire fulfills its own secret desire to obliterate itself, and into the vacuum rush those fragmented objects cut off from human life that are in a sense the leftover traces of desire. At the end of Balzac's story "M. Gobseck," Gobseck's rooms are thrown open, and the debris he collected in the final months of his life is revealed: moldy and decayed food, half-eaten by rats and swarming with maggots, along with furniture, bales of cotton, casks of sugar, rum, coffee, and tobacco, lamps and plate, and so forth. The passage is a powerful image of dead matter and waste, and of money's transformation of desire into disgust.[2]

But money is also, as Lionel Trilling says, "the great generator of illusion" in novels.[3] In a world where paper is gradually coming to substitute for gold, money itself is a dream, a fiction. With paper, the representation of wealth itself becomes a form of wealth, so that, as J. Hillis Miller points out, "the appearance of money is as good as really possessing it."[4] So the Lammles in *Our Mutual Friend*, Becky and Rawdon

---

[2]The irony of "M. Gobseck" is also this: that the miser who loves gold because it doesn't perish has also hoarded perishable things, which in fact have begun to decay.

[3]Lionel Trilling, *The Liberal Imagination* (New York: Doubleday, 1953), p. 203.

[4]Afterword to *Our Mutual Friend* (New York: Signet Classics, 1964), p. 904. Compare Trilling: "To appear to be established is one of the ways of becoming established." *Liberal Imagination*, p. 204.

The Revenge of the Material

Crawley in *Vanity Fair*, Melmotte in *The Way We Live Now*, or Merdle in *Little Dorrit* live almost entirely upon the credit extended to them because they present the appearance of wealth. But in all cases the bubble bursts. In its double character of the illusory and the real, money has the power to alter appearances by robbing them of their material base; it can turn reality into dream, but it can also turn dream into reality. One of the typical ways reality closes in on appearances in the realistic novel is the seizure and sale of a character's possessions to satisfy creditors. This occurs so often that we may recognize in it one of the collective nightmares of the middle class in the nineteenth century. It happens in *Our Mutual Friend*, *L'éducation sentimentale*, Thackeray's *The History of Samuel Titmarsh* and *Vanity Fair*, *The Mill on the Floss*, *David Copperfield*, *The Mayor of Casterbridge*, and *The Princess Casamassima*; it threatens often in Balzac; and it is barely averted in *Dombey and Son*, *Framley Parsonage*, *Middlemarch*, and *Madame Bovary*. Possessions in such instances become reduced to mere objects, raw material; they are signs no longer of the social but of the physical world. "After that they sold her dresses, then one of her hats with a limp, broken feather, then her furs, then three pairs of shoes; and the distribution of these relics, which vaguely recalled the shape of her limbs, struck him as an atrocity, as if he were watching crows tearing her corpse to pieces" (*L'éducation sentimentale*).[5] A similar scene occurs in Norris's *McTeague*. In both novels, in being displaced from their arrangement in a domestic round of activities and spaces, objects assume their implicit discreteness. They become pieces, atoms, debris, or in the case of Flaubert (ironically, of course) relics.

As a representation of material existence in fiction, money always has this double aspect: it is the dreams and illusions of characters, their world of appearances, and undermining this

[5]The translation of *L'éducation sentimentale*, *Sentimental Education*, is by Robert Baldick (Harmondsworth: Penguin Books, 1964).

it is the world of sordid reality. Money encompasses these two poles, but little in between. This split is of course implicit in fiction from the beginning, in *Don Quixote*, but in the nineteenth century it becomes much more pronounced. It is a split between the material and the immaterial worlds, between matter become dense, visible, and inert and all that matter has excluded in order to become so. Thus money becomes an ironic substitute for that discredited spiritual world displaced by matter; it becomes a religion, a god, and it makes one's fortune, in both senses, the way the gods once did. To have money is to be virtuous, respectable, worthy; not to have it is to be base. "An income of a hundred thousand francs provides a very pretty commentary on the catechism and gives us wonderful help for putting a stock-exchange valuation on moral principles!" says Raphael in *La peau de chagrin*. "Vice for me," he continues, "means living in a garret, wearing threadbare clothes, a grey hat in winter and owing money to the concierge." In realistic fiction, the material and the immaterial exist in inverse proportion to each other: as one shrinks the other expands. Of course the material world is far more suited to the novelist's powers of description. Hence genuine virtue often seems shallow and sentimental in Balzac as well as in Dickens. In Balzac it dwells in a world apart, like a nunnery surrounded by gaming houses and brothels.

If money is religion or a substitute for religion, then the split between the material and immaterial worlds, between the low and the high, the sordid and the lofty exists by virtue of the secret link between them: money. Numerous characters in fiction reveal this: Pip in *Great Expectations*, Dorrit in *Little Dorrit*, Emma in *Madame Bovary*, Bulstrode in *Middlemarch*, and any number of characters in Henry James and Balzac.[6]

[6]Cf. Edward Said: "Both Dickens in *Great Expectations* and Flaubert in *Madame Bovary* use money to signify the protagonists' transitory power to shore up their authority to dream and even for a while to be something they cannot long remain being." *Beginnings* (New York: Basic Books, 1975), p. 98.

"When the money slides into the young man's pocket," says Balzac in *Le Père Goriot*, "an imaginary column is created for his support. He carries himself better than he did before, he meets your eye directly, his movements are more agile. . . . In short the bird that was wingless has found its powers."[7] This is similar to the language James uses in *The Portrait of a Lady* and *The Wings of the Dove*. "Spread your wings," Ralph says to Isabel Archer. "Rise above the ground." In *The Portrait of a Lady*, money emanates from the sick and old and corrupts the young and innocent. It doesn't matter that the sick and old are themselves innocent and naive (if a bit dangerous, like overgrown children)—money comes from them, and money is sordid. They want Isabel to soar, and instead she lands in the mud. Over and over again nineteenth-century novelists play variations on this theme. Characters soar on wings of money and land in the muck of material reality. For example, the wonderful scene in *Great Expectations* in which Pip, decked out like a gentleman, encounters Trabb's boy on the street:

> Deeming that a serene and unconscious contemplation of him would best beseem me, and would be most likely to quell his evil mind, I advanced with that expression of countenance, and was rather congratulating myself on my success, when suddenly the knees of Trabb's boy smote together, his hair uprose, his cap fell off, he trembled violently in every limb, staggered out into the road, and crying to the populace, "Hold me! I'm so frightened!" feigned to be in a paroxysm of terror and contri-

[7] The translation of *Le Père Goriot* is by E. K. Brown (New York: Modern Library, 1950). Compare these nearly identical passages in Trollope and Gissing. The first is from *The Small House at Allington*: "Moneys in possession or in expectation do give a set to the head, and a confidence to the voice, and an assurance to the man, which will help him much in his walk in life." The second is from *New Grub Street*: "Money is a great fortifier of self-respect. Since she had become really conscious of her position as the owner of five thousand pounds, Marian spoke with a steadier voice, walked with a firmer step."

tion, occasioned by the dignity of my appearance. As I passed him, his teeth loudly chattered in his head, and with every mark of extreme humiliation, he prostrated himself in the dust.

The gap between Pip's "serene and unconscious contemplation" and the dust where Trabb's boy grovels is there from the beginning of *Great Expectations*. It exists in Miss Havisham's house, but Pip doesn't recognize it, being blinded by Estella's beauty. Its most powerful form is in the relationship between Pip and his secret benefactor, Magwitch. Magwitch's money makes Pip a gentleman, and as a gentleman he is by definition worthy and respectable. But when Magwitch turns up, the gap between the high and low is shown for a moment to be a link, and it is a link Pip cannot abide. His rejection of the convict's money as a first act of moral courage is convincing precisely because money has been shown to be touching everything. Still, it is also an act of moral snobbery, since even Magwitch proves to be not what he seems.

Nineteenth-century fiction is filled with Magwitches and Gobsecks, outcasts of society firmly in control of those who blithely or desperately regard money as a privilege. Bulstrode and Raffles in *Middlemarch* are George Eliot's Pip and Magwitch. Money confers power on the powerless, though the limits of such power are also contained within money.[8] The theme of the high and the low is a direct outgrowth of the two faces of money we have been exploring in this chapter—money as abstract or illusory, and money as matter—and it deserves more attention before we turn to my chief examples, Balzac and Flaubert. Dickens's other great novel on the theme

[8]Cf. Edward Said: "Although the novel itself licenses Pip's expectations, it also mercilessly undercuts them, mainly by showing that these expectations are inherently self-limiting. . . . The more Pip believes he is acting on his own, the more tightly he is drawn into an intricate web of circumstances that weighs him down completely; the plot's progressive revelation of accidents connecting the principal characters is Dickens's method of countering Pip's ideology of free upward progress." *Beginnings*, p. 90.

is *Little Dorrit*, whose two-part division (Book the First, *Poverty*, and Book the Second, *Riches*) is intended to establish a contrast between low and high that can repeatedly be exploited as a similarity. For example, in the eyes of Little Dorrit, now wealthy, Venice's tourist society becomes an imitation of her former life in the debtor's prison, the Marshalsea:

> It appeared on the whole, to Little Dorrit herself, that this same society in which they lived, greatly resembled a superior sort of Marshalsea. Numbers of people seemed to come abroad, pretty much as people had come into the prison; through debt, through idleness, relationship, curiosity, and general unfitness for getting on at home. They were brought into these foreign towns in the custody of couriers and local followers, just as the debtors had been brought into the prison. They prowled about the churches and picture-galleries, much in the old, dreary, prison-yard manner. They were usually going away again tomorrow or next week, and rarely knew their own minds, and seldom did what they said they would do, or went where they said they would go: in all this again, like the prison debtors.

Behind the apparent (and sentimental) suggestion here that there is no real difference between poverty and wealth lies a subtler theme: that just as "reality" defines itself with difficulty against dream (Which is real, the Marshalsea or Venice?), so poverty defines itself not against wealth, but against the material appearance of wealth—again, with difficulty. Mrs. General, for example, is hired by Mr. Dorrit to produce in his family the varnished surface of wealth, and her function reminds us of the Veneerings's dining room in *Our Mutual Friend*, or of Pip's pride in his appearance in *Great Expectations*. To have money is to display money, to triumph conspicuously over others (as in Veblen) by means of appearances. But beneath the varnish, the wealthy are just as constrained by their manners and their dreary routines—by the obligations wealth thrusts upon them—as the debtors in the Marshalsea. The suggestion that the forms of wealth under capitalism are imprisoning is clear. Wealthy, the Dorrits become indebted to an image of themselves just as ruthless in its constraints as the walls of the Marshalsea, and far more threatening too, because "good" society turns out to be swarming with people capable of embarrassing them with reminders of their former position.

As in *Great Expectations*, money in *Little Dorrit* serves the purposes of both irony and romance. The novel is "realistic" in the most common sense, as a story of characters who fail (mostly financially), whose lives are a downward curve, but it is also one of those improbable romances of success, of finding, being given, or marrying into a treasure. And, as in *Great Expectations*, the hidden links between poverty and wealth assert themselves all the more forcibly the more the characters attempt to effect an absolute separation between the two states. The dream of poverty is wealth, and the nightmare of wealth is poverty. Because wealth contains its own loss—a kind of trapdoor through which the money may disappear (Merdle's financial bubble is the novel's paradigm of this)— the Dorrits spurn with paranoid desperation all reminders of their former state. They even turn their backs on Clennam, who in a sense is this novel's congenial, more well-bred Magwitch, the one who in assisting their transition from low to high is in their eyes discredited, not elevated, by his efforts— precisely because of his connection with their poverty. All of this finds its climax in one of the great scenes in nineteenth-century fiction, Mr. Dorrit's "Ladies and gentlemen, welcome to the Marshalsea" speech, delivered in his delirium at a formal dinner in high society in Rome (in fact, a farewell dinner for Mrs. Merdle, whose husband's financial schemes are about to collapse in London). In this scene the low finally overtakes the high, and Mr. Dorrit's fear of being embarrassed by someone from his past is confirmed—but the someone turns out to be himself. This image of the low, as it were, appropriating the high from within is subsequently echoed by that of the faceless Merdle, who in death is described as having "an ob-

tuse head, and coarse, mean, common features." Of course we
are intended to conclude from this that Merdle was corrupt;
but Dickens's metaphor has to do with social class—"common." Dickens's own ambivalence about poverty is reflected
in the contradictory valuations of the low in *Little Dorrit*. The
low is surely something "common" and sordid, like Merdle's
face. But strangely enough, it is also a lost paradise, a lost
home—the Marshalsea—a place where Dorrit and his daughter were once affectionate and close. Only in Dickens could
such a startling reversal grow so naturally out of the premises
of the text: the shades of the prison house are the home we
have lost, not the world that closes around us. On the other
hand, in the world that closes around us the prison has found
its reflection—the world has truly become a prison—in the
sham homes we have created with money, the best example of
which is Merdle's house in Cavendish Square.

Little Dorrit finds its unlikely echo in the century's last great
novel of the high and low, James's *The Princess Casamassima*, in
which a prison also plays a significant role. Like Dickens,
James discovered that the contrast between high and low provided for his middle-class audience a bold sense of drama: the
contrast, for example, between the greasy, murky, festering
cockpits of London with which Book Second ends—the
worm's eye view of London, to use Braudel's phrase[9]—and
the Princess's country estate (Medley Hall) with which Book
Third begins. As in Dickens, the high and the low find their
ironic reflections in each other: Hyacinth Robinson, the lowly
bookbinder with (possibly) aristocratic blood, becomes attracted to the artistic and architectural wonders of Europe,
while his friend the Princess gives her money away to revolu-

[9]"The London drama—its festering criminality, its underworld, its difficult biological life—can only really be comprehended from this worm's eye
view of the poor." Fernand Braudel, *The Structures of Everyday Life: The
Limits of the Possible*, vol. 1 of *Civilization and Capitalism, 15th–18th Century*,
trans. Miriam Kochan and Siân Reynolds (New York: Harper and Row,
1981), p. 555.

tionaries, rents a shabby little house, and fills it with tasteless petit bourgeois bric-a-brac. Hyacinth and the Princess find in each other the qualities each wants to shun but cannot—the low and the high—and as a result they wind up, like Mr. Dorrit before and Mr. Dorrit after, mirroring what each perceives to be his or her own worst side.

The split beween the high and the low was a rich theme for the novel only as long as it could shun Gnosticism, that is, as long as the *links* between high and low could also be revealed. But with the growing sense of physical objects as reductively material, this became less possible. Repeatedly in the nineteenth-century novel we witness the revenge material reality takes upon a morality that regards it as fallen, unredeemed. The final image of Zola's *Nana* is the death blow, not the triumph, of realism, for in this portrait of physical disgust and corruption—the human face not merely as coarse, mean, and common but as rotten meat—the dialectic is stilled, and matter can only decay, can only break down into the "lower" states implicitly present in all its organizations. The trajectory from realism to naturalism completes its course in the theme of entropy, in Beckett and Pynchon in the twentieth century. Of course, we can see the process just beginning in *Persuasion:* the implicit threat of Mr. Elliot's hammer (though never carried out) is that it will break beautiful objects down into chunks of matter. But a better example is perhaps Balzac, in whom objects first explicitly lay siege to the novel's world.

In Balzac there is always a strange world of matter that exists in a sense on either side of reality. It is a series of pictures in a tour guide, a series of economic relationships, but it is also as sordid and cold as clay. It is what is left over when an object's price has been named, the superfluity of matter in its public state, the shell of material appearances: flaking paint on chairs and mantlepieces, threadbare coats, crumbling, worn, and pock-marked friezes and facades. This world of matter is actually abstract, since it usually leaves an aftertaste of reality, a sign of the place where reality used to dwell. It is the shadow of the real world; within it Balzac's characters act out their ambitions and desires. These ambitions and desires alone are real—that is, autonomous, substantial, and in possession of a life, will, and necessity of their own. Never before and perhaps never since has there been such a sheer abundance of objects in literature, and never have objects been so carefully articulated. Still, they often seem fake, as if the world were papier mâché. Balzac is always telling us what objects are made of, as though they couldn't be made of themselves. Curtains are made of silk, hinges of brass, dishes of china, floors of wood or tile, and so forth. He is profoundly conscious of materials, as the long digressions on paper manufacture in *Illusions perdues* demonstrate. Objects have a double nature in Balzac: they are a face presented to the world, and they are a material from which the face is shaped. This view of objects is new to literature—again, largely because of the Industrial Revolution—but implicit in Western culture in Aristotle's notions of form and matter and Locke's primary and secondary qualities. Often in Balzac, the face an object presents to the world is wearing away, and the object has begun to assert itself as sheer matter. "Above the arch a long frieze represented the four seasons by figures carved in hard stone but already corroded and blackened." "There, worn and blackened window sills appear, their delicate carvings scarcely visible" (both examples from *Eugénie Grandet*).[10] As objects break down and their faces wear away, their material nature steps forth and they become present, visible, heavy, dense, no longer part of the normal social flow. In *Splendeurs et misères des courtisanes*, Asia deals in splendid gowns that ladies have been forced to sell to obtain money; they are "no longer gowns but are not yet rags."[11] They are illegible—not signs of wealth,

---

[10]The translation of *Eugénie Grandet* is by Dorothea Walter and John Watkins (New York: Modern Library, 1950).

[11]The translation of *Splendeurs et misères des courtisanes*, *A Harlot High and Low*, is by Rayner Heppenstall (Harmondsworth: Penguin Books, 1970).

but not signs of poverty either. This is a fascinating no-man's-land for Balzac, since objects for him are usually windows through which one views money, or the lack of it ("Paris porters take things in at a glance; they never stop decorated gentlemen of heavy gait who wear blue uniforms. In other words, they recognize money when they see it"—*La Cousine Bette*).[12]

Objects in Balzac are a transparent facade, and they are opaque material reality. "In the drawing room the furniture was upholstered in shabby cotton velvet, plaster statuettes masquerading as Florentine bronzes, a badly carved sconce, merely painted, with molded glass candle-rings, a carpet whose cheapness was belatedly explaining itself in the quantity of cotton used in its manufacture, which had become visible to the naked eye. . . . That horrible room, where everything sagged, where dirty socks hung on the chairs stuffed with horse-hair, whose brown flowers reappeared outlined in dust" (*La Cousine Bette*). Objects present a face, but at the same time the face is peeling, flaking, worn through, no longer adequate to the job of illusion; thus, objects are emblems both of sham and of the poverty of sheer unredeemed material reality beneath the sham.

In a sense Balzac's world is one in which solid things are breaking down and being replaced by their paper representations, just as gold is being replaced by bank notes. It is a material world emptied of value and becoming an image of itself, a shell. Neither the paper image nor the lost reality has any redeeming qualities. Paper is always unstable in Balzac; bank notes and notes of hand are continually discounted and devalued, and the reader always senses their immanent worthlessness. A variation of this theme is David Séchard's search in *Illusions perdues* for a process to manufacture cheap paper: "He had to invent a cheap paper, and that promptly; he had also to

[12]The translation of *La Cousine Bette*, *Cousin Bette*, is by Kathleen Raine (New York: Modern Library, 1958).

The Revenge of the Material

adapt the profits from the discovery to the needs of the household and his business."[13] One feels that he is trying to invent a cheap money, like John Law in the eighteenth century. Similarly, literature in *Illusions perdues* is being replaced by journalism, which Balzac makes clear is nothing more than cheap writing—throwaway words.

Occasionally the paper peels back and we glimpse something underneath. This is a favorite image in Balzac: tarnished or worn or peeling surfaces that show glimpses of objects in their former states. In this sense reality in Balzac is often the nostalgia for reality. Paper representations cover a dense materiality that is a kind of distant lost world, a lost home. Misers hoarding their gold have reverted to that lost world. Gold for the miser actually becomes a kind of manna, in the language of anthropologists, a primitive thriving substance with a magical life of its own. "Really coins live and swarm like men," says old Grandet in *Eugénie Grandet*; "they come and go and sweat and multiply."[14] But of course this is only a short step away from a disgust with matter, since gold for the miser is also excrement.

Such disgust is evident everywhere in Flaubert. Roland Barthes points out in *Writing Degree Zero* that there is a world of difference between Balzac and Flaubert, and I presume he means at least in part that Flaubert is Balzac perfected and become Literature.[15] Still, this world of difference exists only by virtue of the similarities between the two. Both write about characters who victimize themselves by means of money. Madame Bovary's gesture of tossing her last five francs to a

[13]The translation of *Illusions perdues*, *Lost Illusions*, is by Herbert J. Hunt (Harmondsworth: Penguin Books, 1971).
[14]According to Marc Shell, *tokos*, the Greek word for biological offspring, also came to mean interest in the economic sense. *The Economy of Literature* (Baltimore: John Hopkins University Press, 1978), pp. 93–94.
[15]Though his first meaning is that 1848 changed everything. Roland Barthes, *Writing Degree Zero*, trans. Annette Lavers (New York: Hill and Wang, 1968), p. 38.

blind man while her house and property are being seized is straight out of Balzac, as is the character of Lheureux in that novel, or of Arnoux in *L'éducation sentimentale*.

But above all, Flaubert takes the disgust at material existence that is implicit in Balzac and makes it explicit. Balzac has sufficient energy and even goodwill that such disgust still seems to play a secondary role. In Flaubert it pervades every page and becomes inseparable from the cold light in which his language bathes everything. Material things are usually the sign of material imperfection—grease spots, drops of sweat, moles, pores, stains, patches of raw skin, bad breath, heavy folds of cloth, and so on.

> He tucked the catechism into his pocket and stood swinging the heavy vestry key with his hand.
> The setting sun glowing down on his face bleached his woolen cassock. It was shiny at the elbows and frayed at the hem. Grease spots and tobacco followed the line of small buttons down his broad chest. There was a great accumulation of them near his clerical bands, on which the abundant folds of his red skin were resting. His complexion was dotted with yellow blemishes that disappeared under the stubble of his graying beard. He had just had his evening meal and was breathing heavily.[16]

This is realism, but it is also a highly selective vision, like that, for example, in the photographs of Diane Arbus. Its inevitable culmination lies in images of dismemberment and death: the amputation of Hippolyte's leg in *Madame Bovary* after Bovary's farcical operation to correct his clubfoot, the dead baby whose portrait is painted in *L'éducation sentimentale*, the bailiff's fingers "as soft as slugs" in *Madame Bovary*, and the stream of black liquid that flows out of the dead Emma's mouth. As

[16]The translation of *Madame Bovary* is by Mildred Marmur (New York: Signet Classics, 1964).

Sartre points out throughout *L'idiot de la famille*, all of this is symptomatic of extreme self-loathing by Flaubert. It is a self-loathing that in Zola finds its echo in Nana's dead face and in the twentieth century is expressed in the climatic moment of Joyce's "Clay," in Beckett's images of bodily disgust, and in Sartre himself by the nausea his character Roquentin feels at the sheer materiality of objects.

Fredric Jameson sees in Flaubert a lack of the Real, of "that which resists desire," because in fact desire has been replaced by *bovarysme*, the "'desire to desire' whose objects have become illusory images."[17] In a sense this is correct, but perhaps it is misleading as stated. In Flaubert the social and the physical worlds have collapsed together, allowing the latter's sordid or "greasy" quality to become not an object of desire but an object of loathing, an occasion for shutting one's eyes and dreaming one's dreams. As we shall see, this collapse of the social and material becomes inevitable the further down one goes on the social scale. In Gissing and Zola, for example (as in American society today), most social relations center on the workplace. For Flaubert's bourgeoisie, the case is slightly more ambiguous. Social relations are dominated by hypocrisy because they mask material needs and desires, most of them petty. The material world thus becomes a comment upon the illusory freedom of those who pretend to disregard it, and the social world becomes subject to a downward movement as inevitable as the laws of physics.

"Greasy," by the way, applied to the material, became a favorite word of the naturalists who followed on Flaubert's heels (in French, *graisseux* or *gras*). We shall encounter it again in the writer whose world *seems* most greaseless, Henry James. The word itself contains associations that play variations upon the theme of high and low. Grease reminds us of those who cook their food in grease or oil (hence the American word

---

[17]Fredric Jameson, *The Political Unconscious* (Ithaca: Cornell University Press, 1981), p. 184.

"greaser") and thus applies to Mediterranean peoples, those darker, poorer, and more idle races who live below the cooler-headed northern Europeans. In Zola's *L'assommoir*, two of the principal characters, Gervaise and Lantier, come from a town near Marseilles. In Norris's *McTeague*, Maria Macapa is described as a greaser. Both novelists, and Gissing too, use the adjective "greasy" to describe physical environments, and in all three the material world becomes what Sartre defines as slime or stickiness (*visqueux*): "the revenge of the In-itself."[18] All of this is implicit in Flaubert, for whom the physical realm is without value and the immaterial or moral realm a matter of the romantic imagination, no more real than knights on white horses.

If Flaubert (as so many assert) is the beginning of modern literature, he also reveals the process by which one strain of realism seeded its own destruction. The gap between the material and immaterial in Flaubert is finally so great that even money cannot act as a link between them. Given such a gap, the novel loses its ability to deal with the very moral issues money raises, and the social world becomes one-dimensional, absorbed into the physical, a kind of machine. For this reason, Flaubert's plots have an overriding sense of necessity that totally excludes the nervous, energetic presence of obsession and chance we find, say, in Balzac or Dostoevsky.

In a sense what we see in Flaubert is a split of self and world so profound that they simply fail to intersect. *Bovarysme*, the desire to desire, makes of the self a monad, contained within the larger but separate monad of physical reality. The social

[18]Jean-Paul Sartre, *Being and Nothingness*, trans. Hazel E. Barnes (New York: Philosophical Library, 1956), p. 609. A typically sticky description of a physical environment in the naturalists occurs in Gissing's *The Nether World:* "Rain had just begun to fall, and with it descended the smut and grime that darkened above the houses; the pavement was speedily over-smeared with sticky mud, and passing vehicles flung splashes in every direction. Odours of oil and shoddy, and all such things as characterised the town, grew more pungent under the heavy shower."

world disappears in between, and money becomes part of the unobtainable not-I that continually recedes beyond Emma's grasp. This vision of unmediated reality is implicit in certain assumptions of realistic fiction and finds its most powerful image in the figure of the eavesdropper, as we shall see in the next chapter.

CHAPTER FOUR

Reading, Writing, and Eavesdropping

We embark now on a short digression from the theme of money in order to work our way back to it. If economic and aesthetic considerations are truly connected, this should be no problem. The novel is the product of a formal history—of the various shapes taken by the ancient impulse to tell stories—subjected to the pressures of a new social and economic order. Using as a starting point that formal history and one recurring image in it, the figure of the eavesdropper, I hope to suggest a new approach to the idea of realism, one that will account for the nearly monadic separation of self and world in a writer like Flaubert. As we shall see, there is another equally powerful image of this separation in the nineteenth century: money.

The novel has a long list of forebears: epic poetry, drama, myth, romance, history, autobiography, and so forth.[1] Behind them all lies the impulse to tell a story, an impulse deceptively innocent owing to the nostalgia often associated with it. For all the differences between the two, the realistic novel still has taproots in the folktale. Or—to change the metaphor—there are features in stories that come to inhabit novels not

[1] See Robert Scholes and Robert Kellogg, *The Nature of Narrative* (New York: Oxford University Press, 1966).

exactly as fossils, but as if they were morphological characteristics in the anatomy of an evolving species, such as the horse's hoof or the opposable thumb of primates.[2]

A story is a public exchange; listeners gather around the storyteller in a marketplace or other public area.[3] Novels, we infer, are private exchanges, since both the author and the reader are alone. But even storytelling may have its source in the relatively private exchange of telling secrets. When two people talk, telling secrets and boasting are the polar ways their talk can float into narrative. A secret tends to be told in the third person, a boast in the first. A secret is a kind of inverted boast, a story whose concavity invites the listener inside, whereas a boast is something we are expected to admire from outside. Perhaps for this reason the third person came to dominate storytelling, even though the boast never really died out. *The Odyssey* may be considered one long boast, which is why the first person breaks in, something unusual for epic poems. The American tall tale is another form of boasting.

But most stories, especially once they enter the marketplace, take the form of an exchange of confidences about other people. When the narrative concavity of telling a secret combines with the quality of lying or exaggerating we associate with boasts, then stories are born. Stories in fact often verge on gossip, as D. H. Lawrence points out in *Lady Chatterley's Lover*, and certainly this tendency of narrative has never abandoned fiction. First-person narrators in novels often explicitly confide in the reader-listener (*The Good Soldier* and *Lolita* are examples), and such confidence is implicit in any third-person

---

[2]Cf. Walter Benjamin: "The fairy tale, which to this day is the first tutor of children because it was once the tutor of mankind, secretly lives on in the story." *Illuminations*, trans. Harry Zohn (New York: Schocken Books, 1969), p. 102.
[3]See Paul Zweig, *The Adventurer* (New York: Basic Books, 1974), p. 89.

Money and Fiction

tale or novel.[4] The listener tends to believe in the tale more readily if it is presented as a secret about someone else. A secret is a covert form of the truth; in secrets, truth and shame come together. We could even say that a secret is the truth subject to the conditions of a lie. What better definition of fiction is there?

For this reason secrets, disguises, and hiding places are recurring elements in stories. "Rumpelstiltskin" is probably the best-known example. The secrets in folktales deal not only with human beings and their cleverness or foolishness, but with the secret world as well, the world of demons, ghosts, witches, fairies, and other supernatural beings. In novels too secrets are common and have even generated their own type of fiction, the mystery story, and their own custodian, the detective. Defoe's narrators all confess their secret lives in his novels, which are modeled, according to Ian Watt, on the Puritan confessional memoir.[5] A confession is a secret given the somewhat exhibitionistic quality of a boast, as Dostoevsky shows over and over again. His characters impulsively confess (Grushenka in *The Brothers Karamazov* says, "I must confess everything"), and they even lie in the process to augment the exhilarating sense of worthlessness they feel in the act of confession.

Secrets can play an important role in the plots of novels as well, in part because they are a way information is exchanged, and in part because any information exchanged in such a manner is bound to disrupt a character's life if made public. We can see this in Jane Austen (*Emma, Persuasion*) and especially in Dickens, many of whose novels are sustained by secrets held dormant until the final pages. All the turns of plot in *The Mayor of Casterbridge* are revelations of secrets, as are those in

[4]Cf. Roland Barthes's remarks on the third person in *Writing Degree Zero*, trans. Annette Lavers (New York: Hill and Wang, 1968), pp. 34–38.
[5]Ian Watt, *The Rise of the Novel* (London: Chatto and Windus, 1957), pp. 75ff.

86

La Cousine Bette. Through secrets, characters gain control over each other and begin the process of plotting, thus creating a plot for their narrative. In *La Cousine Bette*, Bette becomes the object of the confidences of the other characters; she is a sort of clearinghouse of secrets and with her knowledge becomes the string puller of the novel, visible as such to the reader but not to the members of her family, who never learn how much she manipulates their fates.

"The principal innovations of the novel, since the eighteenth century," says Paul Zweig, "can be described as new and better ways of telling secrets."[6] Thus the epistolary novel, which gives readers the rare pleasure of reading someone else's mail. If novels reveal secrets, what else is a reader but a kind of eavesdropper? Eavesdropping, exchanged confidences, intercepted mail, confessions, and even their opposites, concealed information or disguises, are all transformations of secrets and secret telling. They are reflections of a storytelling culture in which the contrast between private and public life forms an important element. In the epic, for example, such a contrast doesn't exist, and in this respect the epic may be less important as an ancestor of the novel than is generally supposed. The folktale tradition on the other hand is one that thrives in the nursery, in kitchens, in bedrooms, at hearths, and so forth, and its proximity to the common life makes it receptive to stories that deal with domestic secrets. The contrast between the private and the public is also essential for the theater, that public spectacle in which a wall is pulled down so we may view the king in his bedroom. Many devices of the theater turn upon eavesdropping and secret telling: the character hidden behind the arras, the disguise, the aside, the monologue. In the compressed space and time of the theater such devices are often necessary to enable either the characters or the audience to gain knowledge, just as in the compressed point of view of the early memoir novel (Defoe, Prévost, Cré-

---

[6]Zweig, *Adventurer*, p. 9.

billon, Marivaux) the narrator often resorts to eavesdropping to present us with information he wouldn't otherwise have known.

In the widest sense, eavesdropping includes any situation in which one person perceives one or more others who don't know they are being perceived—overhearing, watching, and even by extension reading someone's letters or diary. Of all the transformations of secrets and secret telling, eavesdropping in this broad sense is perhaps the most interesting, and the one that reveals most clearly the nature of realistic fiction. The true novelist, according to Gide, is an eavesdropper.[7] But so is the true reader, and this is perhaps why reading novels used to be considered illicit. Like a witness, the eavesdropper is morally implicated in an action without taking part in it, but unlike a witness his behavior is tainted. In stories, the character who eavesdrops often experiences a shock because a person or situation reveals itself as something other than had appeared. This happens especially in tales dealing with adultery and cuckolds, such as the medieval fabliaux or the stories in Boccaccio's *Decameron* or the *Thousand and One Nights*. The frame story for the last concerns a king who watches over the garden wall as his brother's wife takes part in an orgy. The peculiar force of such stories stems from the fact that the eavesdropper is helpless—he cannot move, cannot touch what he sees, and is reluctant even to talk about it later. His very silence and his care not to be discovered ironically implicate him in the action. Even recognition scenes in this sense are briefly a form of eavesdropping, scenes whose most frequent

---

[7]In Gide's journal of *The Counterfeiters*, trans. Justin O'Brien, in *The Counterfeiters*, trans. Dorothy Bussy (New York: Modern Library, 1955), p. 410. Cf. Trollope, in *The Warden:* "It is indeed a matter of thankfulness that neither the historian nor the novelist hears all that is said by their heroes or heroines, or how would three volumes or twenty suffice! In the present case so little of this sort have I overheard, that I live in hopes of finishing my work within 300 pages." Gide repeatedly made use of this sort of conceit to give *Les faux-monnayeurs* a quaintly archaic flavor.

version is a character's discovering his wife in someone else's arms. The element of eavesdropping coincides with the shock just before the recognized pair notices the intruder, before they have a chance to run, dissemble, or beg forgiveness. For an instant the intruder feels the same kind of helplessness that all eavesdroppers feel (and perhaps thrill to), the sense of a world framed and yet beyond one's control.

A story from Herodotus may illustrate some of the implications of eavesdropping. The Lydian king Gyges began as a servant in the household of his predecessors. According to Herodotus, Gyges's master was so proud of his queen's beauty that he convinced his servant to hide in a closet and observe her naked. Of course she discovered him. To be seen naked was to be deeply shamed. She demanded that Gyges either die or else kill her husband and become king himself. As Marc Shell shows, the story of Gyges contains recurring instances of the opposition of visibility and invisibility.[8] Once he became king, Gyges commanded that his enemy, Lixos, never see him. The Lydian invention of coinage similarly enabled the public and private realms to bifurcate, to touch only by means of violation. By the use of coins and written messages, Gyges's foil, Deioces, was able to literally withdraw into an inner circle and conduct all his business from a distance, and he thus became (according to Herotodus) one of the first tyrants.[9] When the only connection between the public and the private is the violation of one by the other, the result of course is that both become contaminated. If the king in his public capacity as king has withdrawn into the privacy of an inner chamber, and if someone then observes him, the shame attaches to both. This is because in both cases the observer also knows himself to be observed. Thus the eavesdropper presents us with a species of self-consciousness unique in its con-

[8]Marc Shell, *The Economy of Literature* (Baltimore: Johns Hopkins University Press, 1978), p. 17.
[9]Ibid., pp. 12–13, 17–18.

flation of the private and the public, the invisible and the visible.

We see this repeatedly with that brand of eavesdropping known as voyeurism: the invisible (or private) is made visible, and the visible (the voyeur) invisible. The woman who thinks she is alone is in reality the object of someone else's perception, while the unseen peeping Tom lurking in the shadows lives on the edge of being discovered and made a public object. An extraordinary little tale by Chekhov, "At Sea—A Sailor's Story," doubles this arrangement by giving us two voyeurs. In this story a father and son, both sailors, have won a lottery held by the crew of their ship and are given the privilege of spying on a young pastor and his bride through a hole in the wall of their stateroom. The father and son squeeze into the narrow space between the hull and the stateroom wall and find the hole; but inside the room, something more lurid than they bargained for occurs. A plump English banker enters, and it soon becomes evident that he is negotiating to buy the young bride (or her favors) from the pastor. The sailors cannot hear, only see; the story that unfolds in front of them through gestures is a kind of sordid melodrama. The wife refuses, the pastor sinks to his knees and implores her. It all seems to be happening on stage; the sailors have even drawn back a muslin curtain covering the hole in order to watch. At one point a rat bites the father as he watches, but he must stifle his outcry and mutter curses under his breath. A chain of complicity occurs in this story similar to that in Sartre's famous description (in *Being and Nothingness*) of a man in a hotel watching another man peep through a keyhole.[10] To eavesdrop in tandem, as the father and son do, is to place oneself in the double position of peeping Tom and peeped upon; though they have squeezed into the ship's hold together, the father and son literally *discover* themselves there. The son observes, as it

[10]*Being and Nothingness*, trans. Hazel E. Barnes (New York: Philosophical Library, 1956), pp. 259ff.

were, a belated and displaced primal scene, and the father (who remarks, "You shouldn't see that. You're still a boy") senses the oedipal implications. In other words, their complicity in the act of eavesdropping becomes a sexual complicity as well, a violation of the absent mother's body. And *we* are drawn into this complicity too—the reader experiences the same shock as the son when he realizes with him what is happening in the stateroom.

In this story, sexual matters are not in themselves shocking—they become shocking when placed on stage, when the private is made public, the tickets sold and purchased. Under the character of money, which mediates the private and the public, sexuality loses its salacious innocence, its mythological wonder for sailors at sea, and becomes a commodity. With this knowledge the son knows himself to be visible, knows his body is also an object, like the pastor's wife's. Similarly, a rat bites his father: *his* body becomes an object. Both men learn pain, the awareness that their bodies are things, and in both cases the occasion of the pain is knowledge, the revelation of a world beyond the eavesdropper's experience.

In eavesdropping, two worlds that normally are apart are brought together, but in such a way that they remain separate. In the stories collected by the brothers Grimm, eavesdropping occurs repeatedly, as a way of emphasizing the barriers between a king or prince and the peasant girl he sees and falls in love with, as well as of attempting to overcome those barriers by wish fulfillment. "Rapunzel," surely one of the most haunting of folktales, presents a somewhat more threatening version of this situation. The prince watches Rapunzel let her hair down to the witch on command, attempts it himself, and climbs up to win her. But when he tries it again the following day he finds he has climbed up to the witch instead; he jumps down into a thornbush that blinds him. Actually, this story turns on more than one instance if not of eavesdropping, of observing beyond a barrier the object of desire, and attempting to surmount that barrier. Rapunzel's pregnant mother sees some rampion (rapunzel) in the garden over the wall behind her house, and has a desperate craving for it. Like the prince, she is punished—by losing Rapunzel to the witch. In both cases, the eavesdropper goes one step too far by touching the object of desire, and in both cases this is understood as a form of violation. We know well enough that desire flows from loss, but what about that curious kind of opaque desire embodied in eavesdropping whose gesture is normally to hold back from its object—to sustain the loss, as it were? If the punishment fits the crime, eavesdropping represents perfect justice: the barrier we shouldn't cross nonetheless forces us to leave a part of ourselves behind, whether we cross it or not. "You always saw, in this case, something else than what you were, and you got, in consequence, none of the peace of your condition" (James, *The Wings of the Dove*).

Eavesdropping occurs so often in the nineteenth-century novel that a catalog of instances would make an entire volume. Drawing rooms are ideal places for polite eavesdropping, with their hushed conversations between two lovers in one corner, their piano playing in another, letter writing in a third, and small talk in the middle. Jane Austen repeatedly exploited this theatrical setting; the second climax of *Persuasion*—the point at which Captain Wentworth proposes—occurs when he overhears a conversation between Anne and Captain Harville about woman's constancy versus man's, a conversation she in fact conducts strategically, knowing he is listening. Similarly, almost every novel by Balzac, Dickens, and Hardy contains instances of eavesdropping. The story of Fabrizio falling in love in the tower in *La chartreuse de Parme* is a kind of transformation of "Rapunzel." It happens often in Dostoevsky and Conrad too; when Marlowe on top of the beached ship in *Heart of Darkness* overhears the two men below him talking about Kurtz, eavesdropping takes on the character of a kind of archaeology, where information comes as fragments of words that must be deciphered and teased into meaning. In the twentieth century, eavesdropping often serves to remind the reader of the nineteenth-century novel; this happens in *The Good Sol-*

dier, in Proust—in the incident of Marcel's watching Mlle Vinteuil and her lover in her bedroom performing their little sadomasochistic rituals—and it is certainly Gide's intention in *Les faux-monnayeurs*, in which, it seems, everyone eavesdrops upon everyone else. In the twentieth century, on the other hand, eavesdropping is also our guarantee that, if the world has an objective character, it must be severed from meaning. Thus Camus's definition of the absurd in *Le mythe de Sisyphe* pivots on an example of eavesdropping; the experience of the absurd, he says, is analogous to watching a man in a phone booth gesturing and grimacing as he talks. Like the sailors in Chekhov's story, we see the man but cannot hear what he says. In other words, the absurd is nothing more than the revenge of objectivity in the guise of the literal. It is realism robbed of the impersonal and privileged—the *authenticating*—camera eye, by reducing that eye to the status of a peeping Tom.

But in the nineteenth century eavesdropping presents us with an image in miniature of realistic fiction. It unites two contradictory qualities, the sense of the objective and the sense of the artificial, or theatrical, both of which are essential to realism. The sense of the objective is simply a sense of the world happened upon, overheard and overseen, not created for one's benefit, not a projection of one's wishes or fantasies. It is the recognition, often frightening, that the world exists without you. Since the characters eavesdropped upon don't know they're being heard or observed, we sense that they aren't acting for us; their masks are off, and they'll speak the truth. This feeling we have about eavesdropping may be the source of the implicit credence we give the third person in fiction. Valéry says that the sentence "The marquise went out at five o'clock" contains the essence of fiction, and what he has in mind may very well be this sense of a world experienced as an object of perception in which perception is not reciprocated.[11] In poetry, incidentally, the opposite is true. An explicit

[11]The statement is quoted by Barthes in *Writing Degree Zero*, p. 31. In the

93

example is the last line of Rilke's "Archaic Torso of Apollo":
"You must change your life." But in fiction, such language
cannot occur except by means of the most radical indirection.
The third person, which sets a world over against our perception, a world that doesn't at the same time reciprocate that
perception, prevents it from occurring. Even when the author
addresses the reader, we implicitly treat him as a narrator, a
convention. The first person in fiction also has this third-
person authority, which is like an office in relation to the
officeholder. The narrator speaks to us, but we seem to over-
hear him. This is because he is an eavesdropper himself. The
gradual development of the third person in the history of the
novel is perhaps simply a refinement of this power of eavesdropping, from the omniscient narrator, the eavesdropper as
God, who can see through walls, to the third person as regis-
tering consciousness, the moral witness of James.[12]

Yet eavesdropping is also a device borrowed from the theater (especially Restoration comedy), and an important part of
its effect is to heighten the theatricality of a scene. When the
sailors in Chekhov's story watch the pastor and his wife
through the peephole, Chekhov's language and description
emphasize this sense of theater. Eavesdropping frames the
world, compresses it, and thus creates an artificial space. Our
image of the eavesdropper always contains an element of melodrama; the desire of the voyeur is to create a sexual drama out
of the most ordinary situations. In Balzac's *La peau de chagrin*,
Raphael hides behind the curtains in Foedora's bedroom, and

---

original French, the use of the *passé simple* may be as important as the third
person: "La marquise sortit à cinq heures." As Jonathan Culler points out,
"the narrator is taking his distance, giving us a pure event stripped of its
existential density." *Structuralist Poetics: Structuralism, Linguistics and the
Study of Literature* (Ithaca: Cornell University Press, 1975), p. 199.

[12]Cf. Barthes: The third person "is the sign of an intelligible pact between
society and the author; but it is also, for the latter, the most important
means he has of building the world in the way that he chooses. It is therefore
more than a literary experiment: it is a human act which connects creation to
History or to existence." *Writing Degree Zero*, pp. 35–36.

his eavesdropping transforms even her sleeping into drama. Similarly, in *La Cousine Bette*, Valérie rises to heights as an actress when she knows her Brazilian lover is watching from behind the bedroom door.

To say that the world is theatrical is simply to say it is a spectacle. It is conspicuous. This is the affirmation implicit in all realistic novels: the world is on display. When this sense of things unites with its opposite, the feeling of objectivity we associate with unanswered perception, the result is a powerful synthetic reality that is the essence of literary realism. Like the world framed by an eavesdropper, the world of a realistic novel conflates the artificial and the literal; it is both exaggerated and compressed, heightened and common.[13] We could even see eavesdropping in this respect as a distillation of all those conventions readers eagerly accept, which enable them to become lost in a story. In a sense, when a writer reminds us we're reading a book, he's being redundant; we always know when we're reading a novel, just as we always know when we're watching a play. The knowledge may come simply from a feeling of discomfort and a sense of being simultaneously outside and within something, like the listener under the eaves. We know it's a story, but at the same time we sense its multiple links with the world, links authenticated by the fact that they aren't a demonstration. Like an eavesdropper, a reader is naturally self-conscious, aware of his perception, but this awareness doesn't prevent him from being fully absorbed into the object of perception.[14]

---

[13]Donald Fanger's notion of "romantic realism" is somewhat similar to this, but I intend my statement to apply to all realism, early and late. *Dostoevsky and Romantic Realism* (Cambridge: Harvard University Press, 1967). See especially chapter 1, "Realism, Pure and Romantic."

[14]Cf. George Levine: "Surely, no Victorian audience ever thought it was reading anything but a novel when it picked up a work of Trollope's or Dickens's. Yet notoriously, much weeping and laughter greeted each new monthly number of Dickens's novels, and people pleaded with the author not to kill little Paul Dombey or Nell." *The Realistic Imagination* (Chicago: University of Chicago Press, 1981), pp. 184–185.

All of this brings up the question of representation, which in turn returns us to economic considerations. One reason for the great popularity of novels in the nineteenth century—one reason among several—may be precisely this greater sophistication of readers, who didn't need the factual guarantee that the memoir or collection of letters created for a story, who didn't need to be told that they were reading literal history.[15] The reader, like the eavesdropper, participates in creating a representation. Representation is not the simple, empirical correspondence between image and reality, but a social contract by which the fidelity of the image to the world is always in the context of *as if* and always entails the reader's (or decoder's) active participation. The parallel with money is telling: paper money comes to be accepted as a representation only when the user's faith in it becomes second nature, part of the way he or she perceives the world. The growth of paper money, like the growth of the novel, is the triumph of a social contract, at least among the middle classes. Both the conventions of paper money and the conventions of realistic fiction constitute a code collectively shared.[16] And like the novel, paper money in the nineteenth century became mimetic: it stood so accurately for the object of desire that it virtually disappeared in the process, as did the mimetic language of realistic fiction. Of course, money never completely disap-

[15]As they often did in the previous century. Cf. Defoe's preface to *Robinson Crusoe:* "The Editor believes the thing to a just History of Fact; neither is there any Appearance of Fiction in it."

[16]Cf. Marc Shell: "Credit, or belief, involves the very ground of aesthetic experience, and the same medium that seems to confer belief in fiduciary money (bank notes) and in scriptural money (created by the process of bookkeeping) also seems to confer it in literature. That medium is writing." *Money, Language, and Thought: Literary and Philosophical Economies from the Medieval to the Modern Era* (Berkeley: University of California Press, 1982), p. 7. Cf. also p. 168: "What confers validity (*Geltung*) on paper money (*Geldscheine*) is not any material property of the paper but rather the authorized statement that appears on it, for example, 'With this you can buy something.'"

pears, just as language doesn't, because both are agents, not just servants, of representation. We might regard the mimetic portraits that eventually appeared on paper money as a belated residue of this agency. Photographic accuracy on a bill came to replace the profile on a coin that functioned by contrast purely as *sign*, invoking the presence of the only person (the king) who could guarantee the coin's value and authenticity. Paper money substitutes the scrupulous (fineness of design and execution) for such invocation; and with it representation becomes, as in a contract, a function of fine print.

When social contracts are given such fragile formal guarantee—necessitated no doubt by a more complex, more bureaucratic society—the possibility of forgery and counterfeiting increases. With paper money, the goal of the counterfeiter becomes not to make something feel like gold, but to make a piece of paper look like a bill or note. This emphasis upon visual accuracy corresponds to a certain visual bias in all mimesis, including the novel, and enables the notion of counterfeit representation to become more general. As long as paper money has existed, it has been tempting to suggest that all fiction (like all art) is counterfeit; indeed, this is a popular idea now.[17] It was introduced, toyed with, and finally rejected more than fifty years ago by Gide in *Les faux-monnayeurs* (*The Counterfeiters*), whose central theme is that the essence of fiction lies in the tension between reality and the representations we make of it. The position that writing is counterfeit is actually satirized in Gide's novel by the figure of Strouvilhou, who wants to demonetize "those promissory notes which go by the name of *words*" by encouraging writers for whom words are the only reality.

But of course words are not the only reality. Like money, they drag things along behind them—awkwardly, imperfectly, but relentlessly. But the very notion that they *might* be

[17]See Hugh Kenner's *The Counterfeiters* (Bloomington: Indiana University Press, 1968).

counterfeit suggests a lingering discomfort with the new modes of representation into which the nineteenth century was being educated. As we shall see in the Epilogue, a most telling example of this discomfort occurs in a passage in Melville's *The Confidence Man.* For now, the figure of the eavesdropper can help us to see more clearly the intrinsic ambivalence of mimetic representation. At bottom this ambivalence is described by Gide's statement: fiction, especially realistic fiction, is not simply the representation of reality, but the tension between an already-constituted world, or history (that which resists desire), and the representations we make of it. (Gide of course intended this description to apply to the novelist's project, but we can see it echoed in the projects of his characters, especially that of the eavesdropper; indeed, the most relentless eavesdropper in Gide's novel, Edouard, is also a novelist and is writing a novel called *Les faux-monnayeurs.*)

The world framed by an eavesdropper is both alien and an object of desire. He willingly participates in the creation of an alien object that by definition exceeds his desire. Why? Economic forms of representation offer, if not an answer, at the very least a homologous situation. Paper money represents a world of needs and desires that, though they may find their origin in the individual, outstrip and exceed him and congeal into an object outside him. Money is power but, as Marx says, alienated power. "It [money] can have a social property only because individuals have alienated their own social relationship from themselves so that it takes the form of a thing."[18] From eavesdropping and money the homology may be extended back to realistic fiction, and it suggests a provisional definition of realism. Realism is that form of fiction in which the I continually defines itself against the not-I, by finding itself involved in ever larger structures of chance and social necessity, so that personal desires and needs clash with the desires and

[18]From the *Grundrisse*, quoted in Shell, *Money, Language, and Thought*, p. 126.

needs of successively larger groups: relatives, friends and lovers, other social classes, other races and nationalities. Running beneath, between, and beyond such groups, the material world provides the ultimate model of resistance to desire. By apparently circumscribing and taming material reality, the Industrial Revolution in fact unmasked it and brought it to the fore as that unmediated world that surfaces when all the social mediators have failed. In realism the commonplace becomes foreign; and we can see realism in the nineteenth century gradually driven to the foreign, to foreign environments and foreign countries, a process that culminates in James and Conrad. The world of a realistic novel inevitably overflows the experience any one character has of it—including the protagonist—and therefore can be recovered only as something both alien and an object of desire. So the difference between a novel like *Robinson Crusoe* and realistic novels dealing with similar themes—the world as foreign object—may very well lie in the degree to which Crusoe succeeds in domesticating his environment. The rupture of self and world is an inescapable fact in realism, though this rupture would naturally require their previous link. Thus the social process in realistic novels is often one of dedomestication, or one in which the world (as in Austen's *Persuasion*) resists being domesticated.

In realistic novels we often find characters who break off entirely from the world around them and assume the posture of simply observing it. Their world becomes simultaneously theatrical and alien. This happens to Rastignac, for example, in *Le Père Goriot*. Rastignac's impotence beyond a certain point—his inability to influence the action—creates in him almost a curiosity as he assumes the role of an audience: he is moved by Père Goriot's death and the behavior of his daughters, but moved like an observer at a play, and he weeps as the reader does at a spectacle he is not part of. In realism, the world is eavesdropped upon to the very degree that it overflows the character's experience. This is what happens to Pierre in *War and Peace* and to many of Conrad's characters.

99

Pierre, walking through Moscow during Napoleon's siege, experiences the whole panoramic and exaggerated world of nineteenth-century fiction with the same intensity and detachment with which a reader experiences a nineteenth-century novel. A similar scene occurs in *Anna Karenina*, when Levin attends the election. In a sense, the most real world in fiction is one whose reality is doubtful and troubled, one on the verge of passing over from the comfortable and familiar to something that unfolds and displays itself as purely Other. When Isabel Archer happens upon Madame Merle and Osmond talking intimately in *The Portrait of a Lady*, this transition begins for her. Such scenes are common in James: the well-known chapter 4 of Book Eleventh in *The Ambassadors*, in which Strether discovers Chad and Madame de Vionnet together, is comparable, and similar scenes occur in *The Princess Casamassima* and *The Golden Bowl*. The Same passes into the Different; this is the reality of a fictional world. The paradox is that the less real that world becomes, the more real it is. It even briefly takes on the quality of hallucination for Isabel Archer.

For the world to become theatrical in this manner means that Isabel Archer (or Rastignac, or Levin) withdraws into a peripheral, excluded, virtual existence. She is reduced to listening and watching. And the world consequently speaks to her in a voice that is not hers; this is perhaps obvious, but it should be pointed out that such an experience doesn't occur in any of the pastoral forms of literature (in which voices are indistinguishable from each other) and usually not in poetry. Only in drama does it happen.[19] Thus dialogue becomes increasingly important in the novel, and its power comes to

[19]Cf. Frank O'Connor: The novel as an art form "is really a development of the abortive comedy of trades and humors of Shakespeare's day." *The Mirror in the Roadway* (New York: Knopf, 1956), p. 10. Cf. also Fredric Jameson, who mentions the recurring use of such theatrical terms as "scene," "spectacle," and "tableau" in the nineteenth-century novel. *The Political Unconscious* (Ithaca: Cornell University Press, 1981), p. 231.

occupy a more and more central position as realism develops from Austen to Dickens to Dostoevsky.

Still, the world we view in realistic novels is often less domestic than the one we associate with the stage. To sense the world as alien or other—as either a social web of struggling ambitions or a physical one of unredeemed matter (the sea, the earth)—is to set a limit on our ability to domesticate the world with social comedy. And this is precisely the excitement and the power of realism, especially in the age of money: that the homes characters in novels try to carve out of the world are increasingly overwhelmed or undermined by it, like Kellynch Hall, brought with best advantage to the hammer. Indeed, this is the theme of one of the century's greatest novels, *Middlemarch*, whose world is not so much a "real" one as a place with multiple layers of reality. Those most at home in it are generally those who remain in "moral stupidity, taking the world as an udder to feed [their] supreme selves." But George Eliot sees in a sense that we all have to be to some degree stupid: "If we had a keen vision and feeling of all ordinary human life, it would be like hearing the grass grow and the squirrel's heart beat, and we should die of that roar which lies on the other side of silence. As it is, the quickest of us walk about well wadded with stupidity."

Thus, some forms of eavesdropping contain a shock impossible to survive. This is why blindness, the failure to watch or listen, is an important theme in realism as well. Even someone like Lydgate in *Middlemarch*, with a sharp consciousness of the world as Other (as a scientist, his search for the "primitive tissue" implies that he views the world as raw material), is not without his blindness. He shares his wife's ignorance of money matters, for example, though not to the same degree. To Lydgate money is something beneath his consideration, a distraction. To Rosamond (as to her brother Fred) it is something others will provide, a form of grace. Rosamond and Fred are still children; for them money is what it is in fairy tales, a treasure, something severed from work and time. Fred's inability to pay the debt to which Caleb Garth lends his signature, and even more his exclusion from Peter Featherstone's will, are shocks that educate him almost overnight to the intransigence of the world. Rosamond, by contrast, seems not to be educable; when she finds that her own abundant goodwill and agreeableness are not reciprocated by the world, she simply turns bitter and even more spoiled.

In both cases money—or more accurately the lack of it—comes to represent that resistance of the world against which the self must define (or fail to define) itself. It is "real" in the sense in which Freudians oppose reality to pleasure, real because it operates as a barrier to widening the restrictive world in conformity to one's fantasies. So the world becomes what one cannot imagine—or, to say the same thing, what one can only imagine. This sense of the world as the limit of the imagination exists to a degree in all realistic fiction and finds its most complete expression in *Don Quixote* and *Madame Bovary*. Emma Bovary and Rosamond Lydgate are actually very similar characters, not only because both are married to doctors, but also because both feel a perfect right to the money they don't possess, and this feeling has its source in a romantic imagination whose self-enclosed world is constantly being eroded by matters of household economy.

We often think of George Eliot as the supreme English realist, the one whose art was the most mimetic, as opposed to Dickens, whose art was the most exaggerated or theatrical. Both were realists in the truest sense, though: they were eavesdroppers upon an alien world that the act of eavesdropping helped render alien. When the world itself (understood as everything that is not the self) becomes an object of desire, we are in a very different age from any that came before the nineteenth century, an age in which the antithesis of romance is not, let us say, tragedy, but rather domestic economy. In this respect Dickens and George Eliot have much in common. Before turning to look in greater detail at the contours of the world of the realistic novel—particularly at the sense of time in that world—it may help to complete this provisional definition of realism with a brief glance at Dickens. If the world framed by the eavesdropper is both alien and theatrical, no better illustration of this exists than in Dickens. With him as with Eliot we can see very clearly that "realism" does not refer to a phenomenon by which the novel suddenly opened its eyes and discovered reality. Rather, the novel in the nineteenth century was part of a general cultural shift that was creating the reality we see in fiction—creating a world in which individuals were forced more than ever to act publicly and conspicuously to fulfill their private ambitions and desires.

The writer who labors under the eaves, who listens at doors and peeks through windows, is bound after a while to regard his characters as unruly actors.[20] Dickens's best characters not only strike poses, make speeches, and wear costumes, not only are larger than life and less than living, they also contain a threat, a warning: released from their roles, they could spiral out of control, could become ferocious in their anger, grotesque and nightmarish in their very machinelike repetitiveness. They could seize the dollhouses they live in and wreck them. Often we encounter a character/actor in Dickens who can barely suppress his more material energies: Bradley Headstone in *Our Mutual Friend*, or the wonderfully comic, nightmarish Mr. F.'s Aunt in *Little Dorrit*, who represents, or rather *is*, a purely contingent force in the novel, entirely unexplained and unaccounted for. Mr. F.'s Aunt speaks either in

[20]This becomes explicitly the case in Gide's *Les faux-monnayeurs:* "If it ever happens to me to invent another story, I shall allow only well-tempered characters to inhabit it—characters that life, instead of blunting, sharpens. Laura, Douviers, La Pérouse, Asaïs . . . what is to be done with such people as these? It was not I who sought them out."

The notion in the following pages that Dickens owes much to the theater and theatrical devices has been explored in detail by William Axton in *Circle of Fire* (Lexington: University of Kentucky Press, 1966).

non sequitors or in bitter invectives directed at only one person, the novel's hero, Arthur Clennam; she does nothing else, and the result of each of her appearances is that she must be led offstage, "conducted into retirement." She appears to be a character who *refuses* to assume a role and thus throws an uncertain light upon all the role players in Dickens, all the Micawbers and Pecksniffs and Heeps and Floras.

Who *are* these creatures anyway, and where did they come from? Clearly, they are imagined as obsessions, as human beings whose obsessive behavior denotes a superfluity of monadic "nature" or "personality," a kind of homogeneous upsurge of being. They are obsessive not merely in the Freudian sense; they must repeat everything they do or say, not only as a ritual of personal adjustment, but as if to call themselves into existence, to establish their right—and their credentials—to occupy the stage. They treat the world obsessively too, transforming it into extensions of their singular obsessions. Miss Havisham's rooms, Wemmick's castle and grounds (both in *Great Expectations*), and the parlor wall of Mrs. Plornish's house in the middle of industrial London in *Little Dorrit*, upon which is painted a life-sized thatched cottage complete with birds, hollyhocks, and a faithful dog, all demonstrate that Dickens's characters shared his chief obsession with a world one must twist and prop up and paint to make it do one's bidding. But of course the props fall down, the paint peels off—especially in the later Dickens. The collapse of the old Clennam house in *Little Dorrit*, literally propped up by "some half-dozen gigantic crutches," is worthy of the greatest spectacles of the stage: "In one swift instant, the old house was before them, with the man lying smoking in the window; another thundering sound, and it heaved, surged outward, opened asunder in fifty places, collapsed, and fell." In fact, this is the spectacle of spectacles, a staged illusion that destroys the theater housing it as well. But the question arises: When Dickens strips his characters of their costumes, or his stage of its scenery, what is left? This occurs several times in the later novels, in a number of ways, and the answer is always uneasy and uncertain.

For example, in *Our Mutual Friend* one of the central actions turned out to have been an elaborate play; Boffin only pretends to be a miser to demonstrate to Bella the evils of money and to encourage her to be favorably inclined toward Rokesmith, who has himself been acting a part since the beginning of the novel. The reader is easily taken in because Dickens's world is so theatrical to begin with that little distinction is possible between theater and reality. For this reason Dickens gets away with quite a bit; we do not question how Boffin, a servant, could have learned overnight to be such an accomplished, even inspired actor (as his wife points out), because we sense he is already an actor by virtue of inhabiting Dickens's world. He becomes sly and clever like an actor, too: he arranges his theater so that a member of his unwitting audience, Wegg, provides him with the material for his role by reading the part to him. These are brilliant and wonderful scenes, in which Wegg, himself an actor but dropping in and out of his role when Boffin's back is turned and nudging or kicking Venus, reads to Boffin from his books about misers. Both characters are trying to transform the people around them into audiences, and the world into theater, but Boffin's theater turns out to be the larger and to be closing around Wegg, unbeknown both to him and to the reader. In this sense Boffin is the representative in the novel of Dickens himself, whose theater closes around them all. Boffin is both actor and audience, author and character, text and reader. One thinks of the historical Charles Dickens, author and actor, reading passages from his novels on his lecture tours and acting out the roles so passionately that he loses himself in them and breaks down weeping.

When Boffin steps out of his role and takes a bow, and when we have recovered from the trick, our first reaction is that Dickens has made a mistake and given us too much of a peek at the artificial nature of his world. But if the effect is to make the real seem illusory, it is also to make the illusory seem real. The "real" world becomes one in which people act and wear masks and manipulate appearances so as to seem what they are not. In other words, this is a realistic portrait of the social world, and in particular an ironic reflection of "good" society as seen in the lower classes. The reader is given a privileged experience of this social world, first by being deceived, then by being made to reflect upon his deception. In a way, the reader's privilege is greater than Bella's (the object of the playacting), since we also see the self-deception of the actors, who think that they can step out of their roles for good or that the world of appearances ceases once the performance is over. In fact, that world has just begun: now the characters must live happily ever after.

Another way of saying this is that, when we learn Boffin has been acting, a rupture is created and our implicit belief in the narrative is shaken. Now the characters have a new dimension: we are conscious of them *as* characters, as fabrications. Yet, at the same time, they have managed to escape our expectations and surprise us. Dickens makes them unpredictable not by rounding them out and setting them free (as Dostoevsky does), but by flattening them and having them point at their masks and costumes. By intensifying the sense of them as fabrications, he gives them a curious kind of independence and reality. He creates three dimensions by stacking two-dimensional figures in front of each other like placards. Between Boffin and his role as a miser, between John Harmon and his role as Rokesmith, a space opens up, and within this space we get a brief glimpse of the objective world, a glimpse that disappears as quickly as it occurs, in the same way the actual space of a stage becomes absorbed into the trompe-l'oeil of the set behind it.

Dickens's world nearly always has this trompe-l'oeil quality, which occasionally unmasks itself. His settings repeatedly disappear into labyrinthine alleys and lanes, diminishing cubbyholes, proliferating shelves, tables, back rooms, cupboards in dimly lit shops, and homes that overflow with leering objects and detritus. There is little sky, little open space; when there is sky, it is painted in foreboding colors and swirling shapes. When there is open space it is filled with fog, mist, haze, or smoke. For the most part, everything is closed, low-ceilinged, tight, and crowded, like an intimate theater in which the audience is nearly onstage with the characters and can see the powder and greasepaint and the wooden guns and chalk marks on the floor. Dickens gives us the definition in literature of claustrophobia: the conjunction of the alien and the intimate. Balzac tries to do the same but never succeeds in quite the way Dickens does. Both often use similar language to describe physical environments: they are prisons, crypts. But in Balzac there is also another world, one in which most of the action of his novels takes place, an airy and abstract world where human desires clash like blips on a radar screen. In Dickens, by contrast, the desires of characters often become absorbed and calmed by his elaborate plots, whose architecture is frozen and still.

The failure of many of Dickens's plots was not always duplicated by his contemporaries, although most nineteenth-century novels were heavily plotted. By heavily plotted I mean we feel as we read that time is thickening ahead of us; time has *already* had obligations placed upon it. In many respects this time sense is a reflection of a new economic order. As T. S. Ashton says, "a new sense of time was one of the outstanding pychological features of the industrial revolution."[21] We turn now to this new sense of time and its impact upon the plots of novels.

[21]T. S. Ashton, *The Industrial Revolution, 1760–1830* (Oxford: Oxford University Press, 1970), p. 80.

CHAPTER FIVE

On Borrowed Time:
The Gambler and *La Cousine Bette*

The beginnings of novels: "It was late in the evening when K. arrived." "Thirty years ago, Marseilles lay burning in the sun, one day." "At about nine o'clock in the morning at the end of November, during a thaw, the Warsaw train was approaching Petersburg at full speed." "It is a truth universally acknowledged. . . ."

Thomas Mann tells us that Tolstoy overheard his son reading a Pushkin story that begins "The guests assembled in the country house" and exclaimed, "That's the way to begin." He walked into his study and wrote, "In the Oblonsky house great confusion reigned," the original first sentence of *Anna Karenina*.[1] Mann himself wrote the ultimate opening sentence in *Buddenbrooks:* "And—and—what comes next?"

For the reader, such beginnings are invitations; they remind us that reading a novel is still an act with its roots in listening to a story, an act whose essence consists of open-ended anticipation. But reading also has the advantage over listening that it can become a little licentious. In a "good read" we break the chain of prose almost imperceptibly and skid across the

[1]Thomas Mann, *"Anna Karenina,"* in *Essays*, trans. H. T. Lowe-Porter (New York: Vintage Books, 1957), p 182.

words. Certain writers encourage this—Balzac, Dostoevsky, Defoe. They seem to dispense with language by allowing it to disappear into its own flow. If words were coins, I could imagine Balzac and Dostoevsky spending them in order not to have them, so they would continue to serve as objects of desire. They are the spendthrifts of language, as Flaubert is the miser.

By contrast, most nonfiction is a form of already-digested thought contained within language, whereas in fiction the world in the language is always just slipping ahead and escaping. A curious pattern in folktales confirms this: characters try to retrace their paths and cannot do so. Children wander into the woods strewing bread crumbs to mark their path, but birds eat the crumbs and the children are cut off, as it were, in their story. In its infancy, fiction always has this disappearing past—Defoe's novels possess this quality. Later on, writers find ways to graft the past onto the future. But even with this grafted time, the effect is not so much to preserve the past as to harness the future. The experience of the past in novels is that of refracting peaks perceived through each other: time folds up like an accordion and disappears into the valleys. This is true even—or especially—in Proust.

The experience of the future is more complex. We do not want it to preexist (as Sartre points out),[2] but the sense of closure in, say, a Dickens novel is often overwhelming. The effect of suspense may well be a kind of surplus anticipation, a desire to overcome the text's unredeemable promise of going on and on even while it is closing.[3] Until the final sentence, all narratives are propelled by a gap or lack—the intolerable lack of their own closure—that, as Walter Benjamin points out, operates like a draft. "The suspense which permeates the

[2]Jean-Paul Sartre, "François Mauriac and Freedom," in *Literary and Philosophical Essays*, trans. Annette Michelson (New York: Criterion Books, 1955).
[3]Cf. the final words of Beckett's *The Unnamable:* "I can't go on, I'll go on."

novel is very much like the draft which stimulates the flame in the fireplace and enlivens its play."[4]

A classic situation in nineteenth-century fiction, one that occurs with the frequency of nightmare, is that of a character trying to find money to pay a debt. Since money usually shrinks as desires stretch, this situation always has an urgency and desperation about it. It occurs repeatedly in Balzac and Trollope and several times in Dostoevsky and Gissing, as well as in *Madame Bovary, Middlemarch, Vanity Fair, David Copperfield, Little Dorrit, Our Mutual Friend*, and other works. A debt is a means of binding the future to the past and literally living on borrowed time. The future hardens into a road with milestones up ahead, and we watch it approach (or try not to watch it) while perpetually deferring our present. The future literally *closes in*. In some novels the sense of guilt and retribution is nearly biblical. As Freud said about Dostoevsky, his "burden of guilt had taken tangible shape as a burden of debt."[5] For readers the element of suspense enters with the obvious questions: Will she find the money? *How* will she find it? Caught in such a narrative, we read with heightened eagerness. Time seems both elongated and compressed; it is squeezed into a smaller and smaller span, so that it heats up and the characters rush around in desperation. We feel the crash coming, sense the imminent doom; yet one more loan, a lucky inheritance, even a gamble or a theft might save everything. When this situation is handled with skill—as it is in *Middlemarch* or *Sister Carrie*—the prose seems strangely to inch forward and to plunge ahead at the same time.

In such situations we are of course no longer under the spell of the first sentence; our open-ended anticipation has encountered complications, and time has begun to congeal. The fu-

---

[4]Walter Benjamin, "The Storyteller," in *Illuminations*, trans. Harry Zohn (New York: Schocken Books, 1969), p. 100.

[5]Cited in Norman O. Brown, *Life against Death* (New York: Vintage Books, 1959), p. 266.

ture now is under compulsion. This is why the narrative moves quickly and also why it moves slowly. At first money worry occupies only a small portion of Lydgate's daily affairs in *Middlemarch*, but gradually it squeezes out everything else—or, rather, everything else becomes transformed into money worry. Each new device Lydgate tries seems to push the future back a little, to delay it, but at the same time nothing delays it. It is inevitable, closed. Still, it hasn't yet occurred, and anything is possible, including last-minute reprieves. So we plunge ahead, not despite but because of the obstacles desire has met. By "desire" I mean a quality in the narrative itself that is shared by the reader and the characters. The drama of desire striving to overcome obstacles is the oldest drama in fiction, and its sense of necessity, as we witness existence being transformed into fate, is the crucial element that engages our attention. We want to devour a narrative that has its own logic of slow inevitability, and we want to do so precisely because of that inevitability, which is there in a sense regardless of the outcome. In Lydgate's case the money turns up (in Madame Bovary's it doesn't), but with such a crushing burden attached to it that he has to wish he had never seen it. Money in fiction often has that character: even when it is grace, it's a curse.

Lydgate's story shows us that a sense of necessity is essential for fiction. The various necessities writers found in the nineteenth century—history, nature, biology, money—are all in a sense substitutes for the necessity the century had lost: God. Behind this assertion is Lukács's famous statement, "The novel is the epic of a world that has been abandoned by God."[6] In the ancient epic, of course, the gods *are* necessity. The surprising thing is that Homer's heroes display such a powerful force of will. In Homer, everything is ordained and given; yet intention, effort, and determination are required to

---

[6]Georg Lukács, *The Theory of the Novel*, trans. Anna Bostock (Cambridge: MIT Press, 1971), p. 88.

carry it out. This contradiction is at the heart of any narrative that creates a strong sense of anticipation. Necessity lends the continuous threat of closure to narrative, and will and desire give it motion.

Necessity is a debt the future pays to the past. If money is the most powerful necessity in realistic fiction, and the most common in the nineteenth-century novel, the chief reason for this lies in its coercive effect upon time, which it alters and restructures from within—which it literally possesses. This is more true as money becomes less materially substantial, for paper money first comes into being in the character of a promise. A bank note is a promise to pay, though, as Peacock said in 1837—in a statement typically mistrustful of paper money—with "paper promises" being issued, "the promise shall always be a payment, and the payment a promise."[7] Paper money, we might say, is a benign form of debt, but its very introduction into daily life signals an economic system in which debt per se is becoming more and more common. As Ruskin put it, "All money, properly so called, is an acknowledgement of debt."[8]

Debt would of course be impossible without calendars. A debt is a means of arresting the future, of quantifying time. The debts novelists enjoy chronicling in the nineteenth century are always harnessed to an explicit time period. "He says he'll let me have one hundred and fifty on a bill at two months for five hundred,—with your name on it" (Trollope, *Can You Forgive Her?*). "But Vavasor before he left did get the money from Mr. Magrium—122£. 10s.—for which an acceptance at two months for 500£. was given in advance" (ibid.). Trollope's novels are full of such details (as are Balzac's) and full of characters caught between the conflicting claims of duty and self-interest, perpetually deferring the future by floating more

[7]Thomas Love Peacock, *Paper Money Lyrics*, in *The Works of Thomas Love Peacock* (New York: AMS Press, 1967), p. 100.

[8]John Ruskin, *Unto This Last*, in *The Works of John Ruskin* (London: George Allen, 1905), 17:50n.

and more debts at ever higher rates of interest. Debt is the chief threat to the closed world of Trollope's novels: it brings in the outsiders, the Jews, and destabilizes one's status, one's privilege. How can one be a gentleman or lady of leisure if one must look everywhere for money? The necessity of money assures that greed, ambition, and avarice will always act as an undertow, washing the sand from beneath firm-standing privilege and duty. Greed, ambition, avarice—these are not sins of a closed world (like the smugness and hypochondria one finds in Jane Austen), but those of a fluid, shifting world, as in Balzac. Although Trollope's instinct is usually to rescue his characters from disaster (whereas Balzac's is to relish their fall), his fears are evident in the recurring figure of the Jewish moneylender, for whom he saves his most opprobrious adjectives: slimy, greasy, low, sneering, and so forth. The most transparent of the century's anti-Semitic novelists, Trollope saw the Jew as threatening because, ironically, he had no past: "The man [Mr. Emilius] was a nasty, greasy, lying, squinting Jew preacher: an imposter, over forty years of age. . . . Of grandfather or grandmother belonging to himself he had probably never heard, but he could so speak of his noble ancestors as to produce belief in Lizzie's mind" (*The Eustace Diamonds*). Beneath such a description we sense what truly threatens an insular society. Money or money hunger represents a sense of time scandalous for a society that thought its chief privilege was to live outside of time—to exist perpetually in the past, upon a landed estate, preferably with a title. Closed time is circular, tied to the seasons, though the seasons in England were thought to have meant for centuries (in other words, for all time) not summer, fall, winter, and spring, but the season in town and the season in the country.

Against this circular time, the new man—the man who spends lavishly, who finds himself always in debt, who literally pawns his past—lives in the perpetual present, on borrowed time. The Lammles in *Our Mutual Friend*, the Crawleys in *Vanity Fair*, live exclusively on their debts. Rawdon Crawley "had a large capital of debts, which, laid out judiciously, will carry a man along for many years." Micawber in *David Copperfield* is similar, though his debts are always catching up with him. Trollope describes the psychology of the debtor as follows:

> That feeling of over-due bills, of bills coming due, of accounts overdrawn, of tradesmen unpaid, of general money cares, is very dreadful at first; but it is astonishing how soon men get used to it. A load which would crush a man at first becomes, by habit, not only endurable, but easy and comfortable to the bearer. The habitual debtor goes along jaunty and with elastic step, almost enjoying the excitement of his embarrassments. (*Framley Parsonage*)

A similar statement appears in *Doctor Thorne:* "How frequent it is that men on their road to ruin feel elation such as this!" Trollope's account of this new man is perhaps tepid by comparison with Balzac's or Dostoevsky's, who relished with greater sympathy their doomed profligates. But Trollope reveals more clearly the central contradiction of a moneyed society that thought it was still a landed society, particularly in *Doctor Thorne*, as we have seen.

The contradiction is also clear in George Eliot. "If the past is not to bind us," Maggie asks Steven in *The Mill on the Floss*, "where can duty lie? We should have no law but the inclination of the moment." The inclination of the moment is represented in the same novel by Mr. Tulliver, who in horsewhipping Wakem reveals himself to be a spendthrift of the emotions. On the other hand, duty is morosely, relentlessly represented by Tom, whose resolve to pay his father's debts hardens and closes him, who binds his future to a past that will be redeemed by the time (in the form of money) he keeps on laying up, accumulating. Jam tomorrow, never jam today.[9] Yet Tom is able to do this precisely because the world he lives in is faster than his father's:

[9]This is Keynes's famous comment on capitalism, cited in Brown, *Life against Death*, p. 273.

"You see Tom," said Mr. Deane at last, throwing himself backward, "the world goes on at a smarter pace now than it did when I was a young fellow. Why, sir, forty years ago, when I was much such a strapping youngster as you, a man expected to pull between the shafts the best part of his life before he got the whip in his hand. The looms went slowish, and fashions didn't alter quite so fast; I'd a best suit that lasted me six years. Everything was on a lower scale, sir—in point of expenditure, I mean. It's this steam, you see, that has made the difference; it drives on every wheel double pace, and the wheel of fortune with 'em. . . . I don't find fault with the change as some people do. Trade, sir, opens a man's eyes; and if the population is to get thicker upon the ground, as it's doing, the world must use its wits at inventions of one sort or other."

Similar passages occur in Dickens's *Dombey and Son* and Dostoevsky's *The Idiot*, particularly with reference to the railroads, which literally sped up time.[10] The passage from Eliot is the

---

[10]In *The Idiot*, Lebeder rants about railroads: "They hustle, they roar, they rend the air with their noise, they hurry, they say, for the happiness of mankind." Translation by David Magarshack (Harmondsworth: Penguin Books, 1973), p. 413. The passage in *Dombey and Son* is long and powerful, one of Dickens's great set pieces: "The first shock of a great earthquake had, just at that period, rent the whole neighborhood to its centre. Traces of its course were visible on every side. Houses were knocked down; streets broken through and stopped; deep pits and trenches dug in the ground; enormous heaps of earth and clay thrown up; buildings that were undermined and shaking, propped by great beams of wood. Here, a chaos of carts, overthrown and jumbled together, lay topsy-turvy at the bottom of a steep unnatural hill; there, confused treasures of iron soaked and rusted in something that had accidentally become a pond. Everywhere were bridges that led nowhere; thoroughfares that were wholly impassable; Babel towers of chimneys, wanting half their height; temporary wooden houses and enclosures, in the most unlikely situations; carcasses of ragged tenements, and fragments of unfinished walls and arches, and piles of scaffolding, and wildernesses of bricks, and giant forms of cranes, and tripods straddling above nothing. . . . In short, the yet unfinished and unopened railroad was in progress." Once completed, the railroad and the engines themselves come to channel and enclose all this disorganized power: "Night and day the conquering engines rumbled at their distant work, or, advancing smoothly to their journey's end, and gliding like tame dragons into the allotted corners

most interesting of the three, however, bristling as it is with linguistic ironies: Mr. Deane "throwing himself backward" (in his chair), the reference to the whip, which conjures up both duty (pulling between the shafts) and its antithesis, the horse-whipping administered by Mr. Tulliver that turned out to be his downfall. The Industrial Revolution and Malthus are also evoked here, as is the paradox of a faster world that is also denser, thicker, that bogs one down. The pun on wheels will turn out to be prophetic for this chapter: frenetic time, as we shall see, finds its fullest expression in the image of gambling and in the century's greatest novel of gambling, Dostoevsky's *The Gambler*, composed in the compressed time of one month in order (what else?) to satisfy its author's debts.

I have been attempting to trace a kind of fissure in the nineteenth-century novel, a contradiction in its sense of narrative time that is also an economic contradiction. On the one hand, narrative closure places the future under compulsion, and this compulsion reflects the increasing preoccupation with debt in both the nineteenth century's society and its fiction. Debt internalizes coercion and links it to older forms of duty, which debt has in fact appropriated. Balzac, for example, solves Lovelace's problem in *Clarissa*: place a woman or her family in debt—like the Baroness Hulot in *La Cousine Bette*—and the assault upon her honor has legal force. Those mutual obligations that are presumably always a part of society and that we know by such names as duty, custom, and manner become, with debt, a means of quantifying the future. The result is the kind of statement Lord Mark makes in *The Wings of the Dove:* "Nobody here, you know, does anything for nothing."

On the other hand, undermining this closure is a subversive sense of the present moment that living on borrowed time

---

grooved out to the inch for their reception, stood bubbling and trembling there, making the walls quake, as if they were dilating with the secret knowledge of great powers yet unsuspected in them, and strong purposes not yet achieved."

ironically strengthens. Against the great, bulky three-decker novels of Dickens and Thackeray at midcentury, with their complexly structured multiple futures, we could set Knut Hamsun's *Hunger* in 1880, in which a pure narrative present, a sense of time continuously billowing and literally getting nowhere, for the first time fully occupies fiction. And between these examples we could locate most realistic novels, whose plots express varying stages of the dialectic of obligated future and disengaged present. Money begins—through credit and debt—by spreading its forms of compulsion across the entire spectrum of time and winds up, like ivy fracturing rock, by fragmenting time, by driving itself into an endless heterogeneous series of broken present moments.

As Balzac's moneylender Gobseck puts it in the story that bears his name: "I like to leave mud on a rich man's carpet; it is not a petty spite; I like to make them feel a touch of the claws of necessity."[11] The necessity of money is nothing more than that of a society in which credit, debt, and the buying and selling of labor place human begins in each other's power. The permutations of this power became one of the novel's most important subjects in the nineteenth century, and the conflict between individual ambition and social necessity was the central expression of this subject. The countless stories of free, clever, willful, groveling, powerful, unscrupulous, and even heroic characters confronted with the necessity of money demonstrate that it is more than simply a theme in fiction—it is something that passes into its very form. Money has to do with the unfolding of narrative, with the time sense in novels, and with the reciprocal play of chance and necessity otherwise known as plot.

The Gambler

In social relations money objectifies chance and necessity, and in gambling this objectification is given the face of a dia-

---

[11]The translation of "M. Gobseck" is by Ellen Marriage in *Father Goriot and M. Gobseck* (Philadelphia: Gebbie Publishing Company, 1898).

gram. Of all the novels that deal with gambling, Dostoevsky's is clearly the most powerful. I shall approach it by way of a discussion of plot and a general consideration of the gambling mentality.

In plot, desire meets obstacles, the obstacles have consequences, time congeals, and the protagonist has to wade through a dense human world that simultaneously laps back on itself and recedes beyond his grasp. The disjunction between self and world we explored in the previous chapter is not merely a given in realism, but the result of an unfolding process, a kind of ritual of separation and (less often and less convincingly) reconciliation. This ritual is plot.

If plot begins in desire, the repeated tendency of desire in the nineteenth-century novel is to channel itself in the direction of money. Like the shagreen in Balzac's *La peau de chagrin*, money shrinks as desires stretch. The reciprocal play of money and its lack and the obstacles thrown in the path of desire by that play are the most common elements of plot in most of Balzac's novels. Even when other factors enter in—love and social position, for example—they are functions of money. One cannot love without position, and one cannot have position without money. Money in Balzac becomes expressive of the very curve of fortune, of the rise and decline in the emotional structure of a story. In *Le Père Goriot*, on a desperate whim, Delphine gives Eugène three hundred francs, tells him to win six thousand, and points him toward a gaming house, where in fact he does win the money. Eugène has never gambled before, but beginner's luck is not only proverbial in gambling (it occurs in *Vanity Fair* and *The Gambler* as well), but an essential element of the open expectations most plots require.

Money sits on the cusp between fortune and chance. At this point "fortune" is a more convenient word than "necessity," because its double meaning contains an ironic play between money as a secular force and money as a quasi-religious force. Money on the one hand is purely secular, subject to the laws of mathematics and economics, and in this respect it is the perfect embodiment of chance. "I don't see that there's any money-getting without chance," says Lydgate in *Middlemarch*, and he is right, at least as far as novels go. If you asked someone on the street how to get money, the most common answer would no doubt be to work for it. But until the last few decades of the century (as we shall see in the final two chapters) most money is obtained (and lost) in novels either by chance or by trickery: by theft, legacies, gifts, loans, gambles.

On the other hand, money is also a transparent medium that can take on all the transcendent meanings the gods have abandoned. It seems to favor certain people and not favor others, as the gods once did. Gamblers call this luck, but they never fail to impute a supernatural character to it. When young George wins at the gaming tables for Becky in *Vanity Fair*, Thackeray comments: "There is a power that arranges that, they say, for beginners." In the same vein, Dostoevsky's gambler Alexis asks, "Is it really impossible to touch gambling without immediately becoming infected with superstition?"[12] Luck is simply chance under the seeming guidance of a supernatural agency; in other words, fortune. But this guidance is always uncertain. Events in gambling have such an ambiguous character that almost anything can be imputed to them, including a necessity they may or may not possess. In a sense the gambler knows this; he knows that there are always two necessities, one mathematical, the other personal, desperate, and therefore supernatural. One of these necessities often serves as a mask for the other, but the gambler is never sure which is which. Only the outcome of events enables him to assign them a meaning, and by then it's too late; if he wins, perhaps the gods were with him, he could have won more, he shouldn't have stopped so soon; if he loses, he should have stopped earlier. This element of doubt, which oscillates be-

[12]The translation of *The Gambler* is by Jessie Coulson (Harmondsworth: Penguin Books, 1966).

tween the mathematical and the supernatural, can never finally be erased. It can only be assuaged by gambling again.

The same ambivalence occurs in plots. It there a supernatural force that guides events? Hardy's characters are always asking this question as the events click into place, pulling
them down. If the novel is the epic of a world abandoned by
God, then plots should not even be possible. Unless, that is,
they find a natural or social base, the kind represented by
money. But regardless of how secular plots become, the sense
of existence transformed into fate or destiny is always there,
so that they never quite lose their religious overtones. For this
reason, plot in the nineteenth-century novel sits on the crest of
a wave whose one slope is supernatural destiny and the other
mathematical necessity.

Thus, one of the central problems with plots becomes the
degree to which they are determined by their issue. We want
plot to open up an expanding web of possibilities; if we don't
have the sense that anything could happen, we're inclined to
stop reading. For the novelist, the experience of creating a plot
is often one of improvising with the given materials, with the
events and characters. But as any novel grows and loses its
innocence, the events and characters crowd in upon each other
to mutually delimit their possibilities, and the significance of
things that do happen is generally determined by the result
they all lead to. We want the sense that anything could happen, but if *only* anything happens we have no plot.

This is a very fine line all realistic novels have to walk,
wobble though they may. *Tom Jones* is probably not a realistic
novel precisely because in its plot chance always converts to
necessity; as Fielding says (not without tongue in cheek), "the
greatest Events are produced by a nice Train of little Circumstances; and more than one Example of this may be discovered
by the accurate Eye, in this our History." The opposite of
Fielding is perhaps Trollope, whose novels bear a resemblance
to life—that is, to the tendency of life to be unexciting and
repetitive and slow to change—that strikes us at times as un-

canny. Actually, in Trollope it seems that both chance and necessity have lain down to rest and events are on a treadmill. For eighteen hundred pages, spread out over two novels, Johnny Eames repeatedly asks Lily Dale to marry him and is repeatedly refused. Such irresolution held in a state of suspension constitutes an imitation of life so dull we can scarcely accuse it of artifice. In Dickens, on the other hand, we often feel that events lead to an end too obviously determined in advance. But this is in fact the problem: the future shouldn't preexist, yet the events must have a reason for occurring in the sequence they do.

As we've seen, in the nineteenth century more and more people had powerful economic reasons for imagining that the future does in fact preexist. In such a society, novels must be constructed so that this congealed future doesn't entirely check the act of reading and leave it without a sense of pursuit. Thus chance becomes crucial for the novelist; it enters in as one of the factors that provide a proliferation of events and a feeling of open possibility out of which the plot takes shape. The future may only apparently preexist, since a chance event might enable it to veer off in an unexpected direction, but whether chance in this sense is the desperate whim of desire— as it often is for characters in debt—or the clumsy tool of an omniscient author, or the sign of the actual formless texture of daily events, depends in part upon *where* it occurs. Novels that begin with chance meetings or chance revelations—for example, *Tess of the D'Urbervilles*—seem to open up the future for a character or set of characters. But novels that rely too heavily upon chance once necessity has taken hold run the risk of tipping the author's coercive hand. Dunstan Cass's literally stumbling upon Silas Marner's cottage during the only fifteen minutes of Marner's life in which he has left it empty and unlocked is a good example. At this point chance has a very different character than it had, say, when it brought the mole catcher Jem Rodney across Marner's path at the story's beginning. It is no longer the representative of the texture of actual daily events, which are seldom functional; rather, it is pre-cisely the opposite, the agent of a pattern of those events. And for this reason we suspect it, we remain unconvinced. We sense that chance has been made to do the job of necessity.

The temptation to transform chance into a larger, more transcendent kind of necessity is bound to surface in the fic-tions of a society in which the future is continually being obligated away. In *Silas Marner* it doesn't work because George Eliot fails to inscribe it into the intentions or desires of the characters themselves. But it becomes far more plausible in the figure of the gambler, because the appeal of gambling is the other face of an economic system in which credit and debt have become so widespread that they have restructured our sense of time. The gambler's project is a special case of the project of the plotter, who must manipulate reality by getting others to do his bidding. The gambler submits himself to the plots of others—to the rules of their games—in order to over-come them by means of chance. He must will what cannot be willed, he must do the impossible, do what authors cannot do without subverting their own intentions: make chance do the job of necessity. The failure of the plot of *Silas Marner*, or of Hardy's plots, or of some of Dickens's, lies precisely in the kind of coup by which the author assumes the role of his characters. That is, the paradox of realistic fiction is that au-thors cannot plot; they must leave that to their characters.

For example, in *Great Expectations*—one of Dickens's most successfully plotted novels—everyone plots around Pip, with-out his really knowing it; everyone is a god to someone else's mortal: Magwitch to Pip, Miss Havisham to Estella, Estella to her suitors, Jaggers to Molly, even Pip to Herbert. Plotting may be defined as acting in such a way that the action is self-perpetuating beyond itself, because it lodges in the life of another actor. It is obviously thus a form of power, even an attempt at immortality, as in the figure of Balzac's Vautrin, who uses ambitious young men not only as tools for obtaining money, but as fountains of youth. Magwitch and Miss Havi-sham in *Great Expectations* are similar. Where such figures are present, the protagonist often has to become a kind of trickster who can improvise his way into or out of a situation. The complexities of plot occur when these intentions clash, as well as when they become entangled with the undercurrent of chance and necessity that usually flows from the wider social world. Because of this undercurrent, the failure of plotting often becomes part of the plot too, as in Balzac's *La Cousine Bette.*

Thus, plotting is a way of attempting to subvert someone else's intentions and substitute one's own. And plot—especially in the nineteenth century—is the combination of this clash of intentions with the matrix of chance and necessity in which they become enmeshed. In fact, as we shall see, chance and necessity in the realistic novel usually flow from that aspect of society that exceeds the individual's reach, that has congealed outside him as an object of desire. A good example of this is the convergence of social forces that crushes Lucien in Paris in Balzac's *Illusions perdues.*[13]

Chance may be defined as the play of necessity. As Lukács points out, the relationship between them is dialectical.[14] The gambler brings that dialectic into the open, into the foreground: it becomes his life. He plots not to submit others to his power, but to overcome a kind of pure chance and necessity that have been lifted from the social matrix, of which they then become the allegory. And of course he fails, as Dostoevsky's novel makes clear. But in doing so, he X-rays plot, he displays—by enacting—its most fundamental anatomy. The plot of *The Gambler* is relatively straightforward and simple, but it gives us the paradigm for most plots and will enable us then to turn to a more complex plot, that of Balzac's *La Cousine Bette,* in which the plotters operate not in gaming houses, but in each other's drawing rooms and bedrooms.

Gambling demonstrates that the notion that realism be-

[13]See Georg Lukács, *Studies in European Realism* (New York: Grosset and Dunlap, 1964), p. 57.
[14]Ibid., p. 56.

comes less real when it comes to utilize chance and coincidence is generally a misconception.[15] It all depends upon how chance is used, upon how it functions, and upon the vision of human life and society that forms its context. Although scenes of gambling occur in many novels—*Moll Flanders, Tom Jones, Roderick Random, The Old Curiosity Shop, Vanity Fair, Barry Lyndon, Can You Forgive Her? The Way We Live Now, Middlemarch, La peau de chagrin, Le Père Goriot, The Confidence Man*—its chief literary expression is in Dostoevsky's *The Gambler*. In *The Gambler*, money is time and money is narrative and plot; yet money is apparently unimportant to Alexis, the gambler of the story and its narrator. When he has it, he spends it quickly and recklessly, in order to be thrown once more into the necessity of gambling. In a sense, gambling ravishes money of its meaning and therefore of its value. If money's source of value is labor (as Adam Smith, Ricardo, and Marx tell us), then gambling gains its meaning and part of its attraction by subjecting money to an illicit condition, that of play. By winning money, one empties it of its identity and eventually even of its attraction. One of the curious paradoxes of gambling is that it reverses the relation of means to end that money itself had reversed in the social order. In society, money is the means to the end of satisfying desires, but often it becomes an end in itself, a stored-up power in which desire becomes anesthetized. Gambling seemingly strips the social order of pretense: money is the avowed goal, the end. Yet this end, money, itself becomes a means for the gambler to continually submit himself to risk and chance. The truly addicted gambler wants to win, but doesn't want money. Alexis throws away his largest earnings (two hundred thousand francs) in three weeks of spending in Paris, and they are the three most boring weeks of

---

[15]For example: "Realistic writers were forced to impose structures of coincidence on 'things as they are.'" George Levine, "Realism Reconsidered," in *Theory of the Novel: New Essays*, ed. John Halperin (New York: Oxford University Press, 1974), p. 249.

his life. Only back at the gaming tables does life take on interest for him again, because only there does the future again become unknown.

But this sense of an unknown future is not entirely what it seems, and in this respect the plot of gambling is similar to that of many novels. Alexis wants to submit to the risk of an open-ended future; yet nothing could be more closed than the necessity of continually returning to the gaming tables. This paradox is a kind of fissure that runs the length of *The Gambler*, but it is also a spine that strengthens the narrative with a sense of obsession. Good narratives often have something of the quality of obsession this one has, and good narratives generally stop at the right point. *The Gambler* stops just as we realize that a mathematical necessity has come to dominate the story and that Alexis's life will now diminish along with his earnings, with strict regularity.

At the outset the story contains elements familiar to readers of nineteenth-century fiction. Alexis is a tutor in a general's household, in love with the general's stepdaughter, who in turn is in love with someone else. They are in a town called Roulettenburg on the German border, and the general gambles every day. Most of the characters are either in debt or in love (the two conditions are not dissimilar), and all are waiting for the general's rich grandmother in Moscow to die. The first shock of the narrative occurs when the grandmother, instead of dying, shows up in town and demands to be shown how to gamble. She is certainly one of the most memorable characters in Dostoevsky, largely because of her churlish self-confidence and pigheadedness, which place her family—anxious for money, as she knows and reminds them—in the comic position of being forced to accept her insults and accede to her wishes. In two days she loses her entire fortune at the gaming tables, and she returns to Moscow broken and bankrupt. Dostoevsky shows brilliantly that the strongest wills—and perhaps only the strongest—are capable of the most resounding acts of suicide. The grandmother serves as a model for Alexis, who goes on to imitate her initial astounding success and also her subsequent losses. But because Alexis is not as strong-willed as she, his losses are somewhat more parsimonious; he becomes the true addict, the one who will string his gains and losses out over time, winning and losing always on a generally downward slope.

The plot, like most, moves forward by gradual accretions that alternate with sudden shocks and reversals. If time is money, then plots always need this oscillating sense of time represented by work and play, the slow and the sudden. In *The Gambler* this oscillation is given an especially appropriate character, since the attraction of gambling lies in the childish wish to defeat time and overthrow work by means of play. But the irony of gambling, as Walter Benjamin points out, is that gamblers become mock laborers:

> Gambling even contains the workman's gesture that is produced by the automatic operation, for there can be no game without the quick movement of the hand by which the stake is put down or a card is picked up. . . . The manipulation of the worker at the machine has no connection with the preceding operation for the very reason that it is its exact repetition. Since each operation at the machine is just as screened off from the preceding operation as a *coup* in a game of chance is from the one that preceded it, the drudgery of the laborer is, in its own way, a counterpart to the drudgery of the gambler.[16]

As this drudgery begins to become evident in *The Gambler*, the narrative draws to a close. Novels usually prefer even the illusion of adventure to the reality of work. The interesting thing about *The Gambler*, however, is that Dostoevsky shows the former gradually eroded by the latter.

To talk about work and play in this fashion is also to talk about necessity and chance. There can be no doubt that by

[16]Benjamin, "On Some Motifs in Baudelaire," in *Illuminations*, p. 177.

submitting himself to risk and chance the gambler is actually surrendering his will to necessity. He is placing it under constraint. The paradox is that he must have a will to surrender. In *The Gambler* Alexis is headstrong and capricious, like so many of Dostoevsky's protagonists, but he is also slavish and menial (he declares to the general's stepdaughter, Polina, "I am your slave"). This contradiction runs all through the novel, especially regarding his relationship to gambling. He comes to Roulettenburg "certain and indeed determined" that "some radical and decisive change in my destiny will inevitably take place." To will something that is inevitable may seem a contradiction, but it happens to all of Homer's heroes, for example. In this respect the addiction to gambling—or perhaps any obsession, such as love in Proust—is a kind of nostalgia for the lost gods, for a world in which one could assert one's freedom and negate it at the same time. Alexis wants to "challenge fate . . . to give it a fillip on the nose or stick my tongue out at it." The will under constraint wants to *feel* the constraint. This is why the inevitable desire of the gambler, just beneath the desire to win, like a hand inside a glove, is the desire to lose. As with chance and necessity, the desire to win and the desire to lose are two sides of the same coin; when he wins, the gambler feels the thrill of robbing fate; when he loses, he feels the comfortable assurance that fate exists.

The will under constraint is a will in intimate touch with necessity, and thus a will that is for a time enlarged and strengthened by the energy of contradiction. For this reason the gambler often feels a certainty that he will win, particularly early in his gambling career, before the strength of his will has been sapped. Walking to the gaming house on the evening of his most extraordinary winnings, Alexis reflects:

> Yes, sometimes the wildest notion, the most apparently impossible idea, takes such a firm hold of the mind that at length it is taken for something realizable. . . . More than that: if the idea coincides with a strong and passionate desire, it may sometimes

be accepted as something predestined, inevitable, fore-or-dained, something that cannot but exist or happen! Perhaps there is some reason for this, some combination of presentiments, some extraordinary exertion of will-power, some self-intoxication of the imagination, or something else—I don't know: but on that evening (which I shall never forget as long as I live) something miraculous happened to me. Although it is completely capable of mathematical proof, nevertheless to this day it remains for me a miraculous happening.

He is correct on both counts: his evening of luck is completely accounted for by mathematics, yet is also something of a religious miracle. Again, *The Gambler* stands at the node, the intersection, between the spiritual and the material worlds. This intersection is a doubtful and troubled place; the gambler feels his luck like a beleaguered Christian feeling the presence of God, with a lump in his throat for fear the whole thing is an illusion. This is why the subsequent narrative of Alexis's winnings is as breathless and exciting as it is predictable, and why it shows us that a sense of necessity in narrative is completely compatible with the sense of the unexpected we associate with chance. Indeed, in a good plot the dialectic between necessity and chance brings both fully into play.

This evening is the high point of Alexis's career. At this point chance is magnificent and powerful. Afterward, however—after Alexis spends his two hundred thousand francs and returns to gambling—chance diminishes, becomes stingy, mathematical, and slowly absorbed into necessity. The reason for this is that Alexis's freedom has committed suicide in one splendid flare, like a comet. When it flares up it is invincible, and the great illusion of gamblers, that chance is in their power, is for the moment a reality. But the triumph of the will is also the death of the will. Dostoevsky even describes the moment of this flaring and death: "There was, however, one instant's expectant pause, perhaps sensation for sensation the same as that experienced by Madame Blanchard in Paris while she was plunging to the ground from the balloon." Chance is absolute, on edge, trembling; the most improbable things happen, red comes up fourteen times in a row, and Alexis continues to bet on it. The difference between winning everything and losing everything is a hair. But of course he wins; in conjunction with absolute chance, necessity is absolute, and both are under his thumb.

And of course he will never win again, except in comparatively small sums, and rarely, as if by accident.[17]

The Gambler could perhaps have been written only at a time of great individual ambition and of the breakdown of the old social forms. These are clichés about the nineteenth century, but Dostoevsky shows their living force. In the midst of an increasingly random world (Mallarmé's metaphor for it is a throw of the dice), the solution is to submit to chance by setting one's will against it, to surrender the will by asserting it. In this way the novel of individual aspiration, which is one characteristic novel of the nineteenth century, becomes the novel of pathos, of the individual crushed by events, which is the characteristic novel of naturalism and to some extent of the twentieth century, as in Kafka. *The Gambler* stands at the point where, as with a ball thrown into the air, one direction becomes its opposite: the point where realism bifurcates.

The same metaphor could serve for the sense in which chance becomes necessity in the plots of novels: one direction becomes its opposite. The sense of the unexpected is stronger in Dostoevsky than in almost any other novelist, yet the sense of necessity is equally powerful. Dostoevsky himself was a gambler, and on the author's authority we can believe his narrator that "in a series of pure chances there really does exist, if not a system, at any rate a sequence." Like Alexis, the reader of *The Gambler* moves from the awareness that anything

[17] I use the word "accident" advisedly here. See the distinction between accident and chance that Lukács makes in *Studies in European Realism*, p. 56.

may happen to the awareness that only this could have happened—moves from the random or unexpected to a system or sequence. Dostoevsky *displays* this process, makes us vividly aware of it; but it is the process of any successfully plotted novel.

Dostoevsky also shows us that a plot rooted in the unexpected is rooted in character too. As powerful as necessity is in his novels, his characters are always willing to give it a fillip on the nose. This is a favorite image in Dostoevsky, an image of sudden, volatile, unanticipated behavior. The unanticipated and the obsessive are the two stools many of Dostoevsky's characters fall between. This is true of Alexis in *The Gambler;* his freedom at the end of the novel in one sense has committed suicide, but in another sense it has transformed itself into the obsession of telling his story, pouring the words forth. His posture in the entire novel reveals itself in the last pages: he has buttonholed the reader and, like almost all of Dostoevsky's characters, cannot restrain himself from talking. Dostoevsky is one of the great creators of dialogue in fiction, and his characters all reveal themselves in talk. When they talk, they lie with the moral fervor of confessing and confess with the narrative precision of a lie; they exhort, become indignant, hide, pose, perform, act foolish, offensive, and slavish by turns (or all at once). One feels that they are simultaneously navigating and being navigated by their own personalities in the act of speech. In a sense *The Gambler* is Alexis's apology in the form of a continuous monologue for the personality he is creating in the act of apologizing. And like any apology in Dostoevsky, it is also an act of defiance. The sense of improvisation and risk in such a monologue is summed up by the narrator's comment on old Fyodor's talk in *The Brothers Karamazov:* "He plunged forward blindly." One thinks of Dostoevsky himself feverishly dictating *The Gambler* over a three-week period to meet a deadline for a publisher who was (of course) his creditor.

Like many other characters in Dostoevsky, Alexis is impulsive, and with the important exception of the grand-mother's visit, most of the sense of the unexpected in the plot stems from his impulsiveness. When he declares he is Polina's slave, she tells him to prove it by saying something in French to a German baroness neither of them knows, whereupon he approaches the baroness on the street and exclaims (in front of her husband), "J'ai l'honneur d'être votre esclave." This is typical behavior in Dostoevsky, and the source of our constant sense that anything could happen on the next page. Such impulsiveness renders Alexis's sudden addiction to gambling perfectly plausible and makes him for one evening the ideal gambler, since no one else, addict or not, would have had the nerve to keep staking red after it had come up fourteen times in a row. Still, by the end of the novel his impulsiveness has hit a bottleneck, and we sense it has grown smaller. "I live, of course, in a constant quiver of anxiety, play for the smallest possible sums, wait for something to happen, make calcula-tions . . . but with all that it seems to me that I have grown stiff and numb, as though I was plastered with some sort of mud." Dostoevsky brings us to this point, but his territory doesn't lie beyond it except in those brief flashes, as on the final page, when the narrator still exhibits a kind of wild, irrational hope and determination.

The Gambler possesses a simple, almost classical structure: it rises to a climax, which occurs three-quarters of the way through the novel, and descends from there to a denouement. As a narrative it is archetypal in the way it unites a sense of the future opened up and the future sealed off, and in the way it roots itself in adventure and chance. It is full of surprises, even though nothing is really surprising, and is supremely suspen-seful even though we know the outcome. Part of its simplicity and purity is due to the first-person narration, which ensures that the essential elements of the plot will involve one char-acter's will in confrontation with chance and necessity. Thus, one by one the other characters disappear, in proportion as the narrator becomes more deeply involved in gambling. With the intentions of the other characters stripped away, the plot avoids many of the complications we generally associate with plot, but it also gains a strength of focus appropriate for a short novel. We can only wonder at Dostoevsky's uncanny intuition for structure, since the novel was virtually created in the act of dictation and went to the publisher unrevised. It is a crude, pure, powerful novel, with its anatomy on display, as it were, like bones under an X-ray machine.

La Cousine Bette

The plot of Balzac's greatest novel, *La Cousine Bette*, is much more complex and at the same time more ragged than that of *The Gambler*, though in its own way typical. In it the intentions of a group of characters clash from the beginning, and Balzac juggles their stories so well that the reader is hard pressed to single out any one character as central. As in *The Gambler*, the sense of necessity in the plot often takes the form of the characters' obsessions—Hulot's infatuations, Bette's revenge—and, as in *The Gambler*, these obsessions gradually become usurped by the need to have money. Like *The Gambler*, *La Cousine Bette* was written hurriedly to satisfy debtors. But the similarities end there; *La Cousine Bette* is a kind of patched-up, sprawling orchestra, occasionally out of tune but with great power and a perfect sense of timing; *The Gambler*, by contrast, is a solo voice in an empty hall.

Balzac spends almost the first hundred pages of the novel in exposition, but the situation he describes is fluid enough that we barely notice when the exposition stops and the plot begins cranking. The fluidity is there because the characters are attempting to coerce each other, for the most part with money. Crevel offers the Baroness Hulot three hundred thousand francs to become his mistress; Hortense pries the name of Bette's secret lover out of her; Hulot sets up Valérie as his mistress; Bette saves Wenceslas's life and becomes his tyrant-protector (and creditor); and Hortense seduces Wenceslas away from Bette. The nervous sense of transition and change in these events enables Balzac to violate Aristotle's definition of a beginning: that with nothing before it. Balzac's world continually overflows itself, and his novels always create the impression of catching it on the run. This is due in part to his recurring characters and stories, which overlap from one novel to the next, but even more to the incessant energy of desire in his novels and the geometric expansion of desires when they intercept and deflect each other like molecules in a gas chamber.

In the exposition as in the rest of the novel, the structure is a series of loosely linked scenes. The link between the scenes throughout the novel is the concealment or revelation of knowledge. That is, one character or set of characters is ignorant about the activity of another or others, and the ignorance is erased by an exchange of confidences or by some form of eavesdropping. Sometimes a confidence is actually a lie, so that knowledge is withheld under the guise of revealing it; in fact, this happens more and more as the novel unfolds, as we shall see. Almost every turn of the plot occurs because of such a revelation of knowledge or a lie. The important exception is the climax, Baron Hulot's fall and disgrace, which is accompanied by the death from shock of the Marshal, his brother, and the suicide of Johann Fischer, his wife's uncle. This climax is largely a result of the necessity of money; the Baron has piled up debts all the way through the novel (in pursuit of his mistresses) and has induced Johann Fischer to take charge of provisions for the French army in Algeria and cheat the government out of two hundred thousand francs. The Baron's schemes and credit all collapse at once, reducing his family to poverty and dishonor and him to a white-haired old man still ferreting out mistresses in the slums of Paris. His story, set in motion by his obsessive infatuations and his need to finance them, is in a sense the spine of the novel, a kind of buried unrelieved necessity to which the other stories are drawn and from which they depart—in fact, a necessity so insistent and grotesque that it continues even on the final pages of the novel, when the Baron is an octogenarian. Throughout the novel, every time we think the Baron will either reform or die, he slips past our expectations and sets off after another woman. Balzac's genius consists at least in part in his ability to make this excess perfectly plausible and even objective, as if he were portraying an especially tenacious organism that refuses to die or relinquish its single-minded appetite.

But if the Baron is the spine of the novel, Bette—often in conjunction with Valérie—is its heart and center. The plot actually begins when Bette learns from Valérie of Wenceslas's forthcoming marriage to Hortense. She vows revenge on the Hulot family, and the two women agree to work for each other's interests—to become plotters. They seal the pact by telling each other their secrets, as if to submit to each other's power. Such secret telling then becomes Bette's chief weapon in plotting revenge on the Hulots. She becomes the repository of all the characters' confidences, and the one who reveals to them, at the proper moments, those secrets that hurt the most (always in the guise of doing them a favor). Her suitability for this role has already been established by her spinster-virgin character, her position outside or on the edge of society, and her silence. "As a rule," Balzac says, "our confidences are made to those below us rather than to those above us. Our inferiors are employed much more often than our superiors in secret affairs; and they thereby become the recipients of our hidden thoughts, they share in our private deliberations. . . . Everyone imagined that this poor spinster was in such a state of dependence on everybody as to be forced to absolute silence. The cousin referred to herself as the family confessional." This seeming dependence that reverses itself, so that at the end Bette is even the Baron's creditor, is one of the chief and most deliberate ironies of the novel.

For Bette, secrets are a form of power. She is the mediator of the novel, but not a vanishing mediator like Anne Elliot in *Persuasion*. We might call her an emerging mediator, one who materializes in the very act of mediation, who becomes more substantial as the novel proceeds. More often than not Bette, in the guise of reconciling a character to the world, alienates him further. She wreaks vengance by giving the other characters the same experience Valérie gives her when she reveals the marriage of Wenceslas and Hortense, the experience of her world and her home becoming Other. Repeatedly she honors the Baroness Hulot with news of her husband's and son-in-law's infidelities, news in the form of confidences (about situations she herself has plotted to establish), and in this way bit by bit she strips the Baroness of her world. Such a plot moves forward by continually dividing the world of the novel and making it more and more partial—by dedomesticating it. A secret revealed at the right time widens the gap between a character and his experience, ironically by pretending to close it; that is, information is revealed that makes it clear to the character that the world is not what he or she thought it was. The Baroness receives those blows as friendly hints intended to apprise her of a situation and make the world of her experience more familiar; but it becomes more familiar only to the degree that it also becomes more alien.

Such carefully hatched secrets are possible only in a situation where there is also a great deal of concealment. The Baron tries to conceal his infidelities, Wenceslas to conceal his attraction to Valérie, Valérie to conceal her various lovers from each other (and the true lover, Montès, from them all), and the entire Hulot family, desperate for respectability, tries to conceal its situation from the Marshal, the Baron's older brother. But once again the center of most of the concealment and disguise in the novel is Bette. Through Bette, Balzac alternates concealment and revelation with such a sense of inevitability that the plot itself takes on a rhythm of contracting and expanding, or of backing up like a log-jammed river, then gushing forth. Information becomes packed into bottlenecks—often in the form of a hushed dialogue between Bette and someone else—and sometimes the reader receives this information at the same moment as one of the characters. These bottlenecks are highly concentrated and charged with potential action, like gun barrels; when they go off, the effect is to send a wave of movement through the plot. The initial conversation between Valérie and Bette has this effect, as do Bette's revelations to the Hulots about the Baron and Wenceslas and Valérie's revelation to her lovers that she is pregnant.

This expanding and contracting rhythm is natural to plots, and to one degree or another it exists in most plotted novels. In *La Cousine Bette*, a doubleness operates throughout the novel that continually counterpoints this rhythm; repeatedly, concealment becomes a form of revelation and revelation becomes concealment. For example, when Hortense walks into her husband's studio, he hastily conceals the mock-up of his Samson and Delilah group, thus inadvertently revealing that he is still in Valérie's power. Most such moments revolve around Valérie and Bette, who become operators (literally) of a central exchange in which information is stored, processed, and circulated in such a way that the false becomes the true and the true the false. There are many examples. When Valérie reveals that she is pregnant, she confides to each of her lovers that he is the father, thus concealing the actual father. In two of the key scenes in the second half of the novel, characters discover their wives or lovers in someone else's arms, and in both cases the scenes are staged, the first to entrap Hulot, the second to enrage the Brazilian and goad him into killing Valérie. In all these incidents the retractile tendency of concealment and the expansive, rippling effect of revelation overlap, and the result is that the plot sends its roots more deeply into the characters, not only into their knowledge of each other, but into their illusions as well.

When concealment and revelation become masks of each other, we are in a very unstable world, a world in which almost anything can be revealed to be an illusion. In such a world, those who can control the instability are those who will

succeed, at least for a time. Valérie and Bette are in control for
most of the novel because each is a consummate actress, a
master of illusions, the one flamboyant and sexy, the other
subdued, speaking sotto voce, and if anything therefore even
more effective. Valérie is the improviser, able to convert embarrassing situations, such as the Brazilian's return, into tri-
umphs. Her greatest triumph occurs when Crevel announces
to her that he will give the Baroness Hulot two hundred thousand francs to save her family. Valérie upbraids him, pleads
with him, cries, declares her love, then coldly drops the role
and breaks into laughter when Crevel weeps before her. "You
great ninny," she says. "That is how pious women set about
pulling up a carrot of two hundred thousand francs!" Not only
does she succeed in completely transforming the Baroness in
Crevel's eyes from a virtuous woman into a hypocrite, but she
does so by revealing her own devices as an actress. The effect
on Crevel is not unlike Boffin's effect on the reader in *Our
Mutual Friend:* he is taken in precisely by being made to doubt
the wrong appearances.

Bette is more subtle, and even more effective. Initially, her
clothing and manner set her off as an inferior member of the
family, one to keep hidden. Later she learns to dress and act
sufficiently well to trap the old Marshal into marriage, a trap
he escapes only by dying. Behind these transformations of
Bette's appearance lies an ability to mirror the appearances
around her. She gives back to the characters their own self-
deceptions, their own lies of respectability, which she alone
recognizes as lies. She thus guarantees and fixes a kind of
relativity at the center of the novel: there is no true and false,
no right and wrong. The characters see and judge what they
want or are given to see and judge, through her eyes. This is
possible in part because the world in the novel is in transition,
so that there are in a sense two worlds, each with its own set of
rules. The Baroness Hulot, the Marshal, Victorine, and old
Johann Fischer live by a code of honor and personal loyalty
that is a sign of the aristocratic class and the older royalist

world; Hulot, Valérie, Bette, and Crevel live by a code of personal ambition whose most visible manifestation is money and that is a sign of the bourgeoisie. From the point of view of each code, the other is false and empty of reality. Bette subscribes to the code of money while giving the appearance of loyalty to the code of honor, and so she is able to deceive characters on both sides of the fence for her own ends.

For the most part, Balzac display masterly objectivity in describing these two worlds and the woman who is at home in both. We know from external evidence that Balzac was on the side of monarchy and the church, but except for Bianchon's speech on money supplanting religion, we would never guess it from this novel. We also know that Balzac himself was fascinated by money, so that even Crevel is the spokesman for one side of the author's mind when he says such things as "I am a man of my time. I respect money!" or "Above the law is the holy, venerable, solid, adored, gracious, beautiful, noble, young, and all-powerful franc!" The two sides of Balzac's mind thus encompassed both codes, both worlds. This is why neither is able to attain a privileged reality in the novel, and why the predators and prey seem to belong to each other so intimately. Perhaps the novel gives us not so much a real world as a world whose characters are continually subverting each other's reality, with their own witting or unwitting complicity. Bette and Valérie may be the plotters, but the plot is eventually shared by all, as an anthill is shared by ants or a bureaucracy by bureaucrats. Thus, as the plot branches out it displays unexpected connections, which are at the same time perfectly natural. For example, the Baron's need for money to make Valérie his mistress sends Johann Fischer to Algeria, and Fischer's need for two hundred thousand francs to avert disgrace sends the Baroness to Crevel, to agree to the offer with which the novel opened. Crevel in turn goes to Valérie, who dissuades him from giving the Baroness the money and subsequently persuades him to marry her. The plot becomes a kind of shared necessity, so that a single movement on the part of one character sends ripples through them all. The reality of the novel is in fact this *social* reality, where individual duplicity becomes collective, and its genius is its ability to walk that thin, intricate line at the intersection of the personal and the social.

In such a tightly knit web of intentions, chance has less of a role than in almost any of Balzac's plots. Still it is a factor, though almost exclusively in the first half of the novel. Chance initially brings Hulot and Valérie together, and it springs Wenceslas from jail just as Bette is savoring her first revenge. In both cases chance is a catalyst for the plot, a spur for the intentions of the characters. The Brazilian's unexpected return while Crevel, the Baron, and Marneffe are all with Valérie is similar and gives rise for the first time to Valérie's powers of improvisation. Once the novel is well under way, however, chance simply disappears as a factor, as if the plot were a machine that only needed a little push to get it going. Few plots are able to sustain movement from within themselves as well as this one, that is, to find their own inner means of propulsion without the need of occasional stimuli from outside. Nearly all of Jane Austen's plots, for example, require the introduction of a stranger about one-third of the way through to give them a push. But in *La Cousine Bette*, with the exception of the Brazilian, the characters are all there from the beginning. One senses in the various movements of its characters a very delicate system of weights and counterbalances that ensures that seemingly idle parts are never really idle but are gathering strength for the relentless push ahead.

One interesting feature of the plot is that, though chance disappears in the second half of the novel, the appearance of chance is sustained. This is most clear in the two entrapment scenes, when Marneffe walks in on Valérie and Hulot and when Montès walks in on Valérie and Wenceslas. Hortense's "discovery" of the letter from Valérie to Wenceslas informing him that he is a father is similar. In creating a kind of theater for each other's wishes or fears, the plotters also create the appearance of chance in order to disguise the theater's theatrical nature. The interesting result is that Balzac thus avoids artificiality in a plot that is full of artificial devices: eavesdropping, acting, plotting, and so forth. The reason is that the artifice is all due to the characters; they act for each other, they arrange the scenes, they write the script. Again, Balzac's objectivity is masterly, as if his characters, not he, were writing the novel. In a plot that flows from plotters, it seems the author need only describe the behavior of his characters, without coercing that behavior or imposing upon it a necessity that does not intrinsically belong to it. The characters create their own necessity: their ambition is theirs, their obsessions are theirs, their downfall is theirs. The novelist, like us, is in the audience. Like Dickens, Balzac shows us that realistic fiction is essentially theatrical in nature, but unlike Dickens he is not onstage pushing sets into place and throwing light switches. Realism is theatrical because its subject is the social world, in which behavior is always to one degree or another a form of mimesis, of imitating behavior.

Thus Valérie, in addition to being a successful courtesan, continually plays the *role* of a courtesan, to the delight of her lovers, who have, as it were, purchased tickets to the performance. Balzac shows that the attraction of a mistress is far less sexual than theatrical; she provides a little drama for her lovers' humdrum lives. In Balzac, courtesans are usually actresses (like Coralie in *Splendeurs et misères des courtisanes*), as they in fact were in nineteenth-century France. This role playing extends to other characters as well: to Bette, who plays the role of the spinster, to Crevel, always posing like a statue of Napoleon, even to the Baroness, whose character as the long-suffering, pious, and forgiving wife is so stubbornly adhered to in the face of her husband's behavior that it finally erodes from within whatever moral value it may have once contained and becomes a parody of itself. At the end of the novel she is almost as grotesque as her husband, who himself is a parody of the libertine, finding younger and younger mistresses as he grows older and older, and purchasing his innocence with the perpetual innocence of money.

Balzac's moneylender Gobseck declares, "What is life but a machine set in motion by money?"—a question we may safely transform into "What are Balzac's plots but machines set in motion by money?" The plot of *La Cousine Bette* is as beautiful a machine as exists in nineteenth-century fiction; I am tempted to say as cold as one as well, but the fact is that for all its air of a medieval morality play, the novel also possesses a strange kind of organic warmth. The source of this warmth is probably Balzac's disinterested interest in watching a splendid set of performers create an elaborately choreographed drama among themselves, a drama complete with ruined families, jilted wives, murder, suicide, and bankruptcy. It is unbelievable, but Balzac never forces it upon us, and so we come to believe in it, which means we come to believe in characters so desperate to make life interesting that they believe in it too.

CHAPTER SIX

Labor and Leisure:
Hunger

When David unmasks Uriah Heep at the end of *David Copperfield*, he can't resist the temptation to lecture the slimy villain. Uriah's schoolboy retort contains enough bitter truth to throw David's triumph into shadow for the moment and previews the unmasking of social hypocrisies that Dickens will increasingly feature in his later novels. "It may be profitable for you to reflect," says David, "that there never were greed and cunning in the world yet, that did not do too much, and overreach themselves. It is as certain as death." Uriah's reply: "Or as certain as they used to teach at school (the same school where I picked up so much umbleness), from nine o'clock to eleven, that labour was a curse; and from eleven o'clock to one, that it was a blessing and a cheerfulness, and a dignity, and I don't know what all, eh?" Uriah's bitterness is the bitterness of one whose labor has not borne fruit, and in a convenient evasion of responsibility he ascribes its blight not to his own greed, but to Adam's curse.

But this is an evasion with a stinger attached. As Max Weber and R. H. Tawney have shown, work and wealth were valued by the Christian West from the seventeenth century on in ways that contributed substantially to the rise of capitalism.[1] Labor may be a curse, but if the laborer can redeem his fallen state by physical effort and material production, he can transform it into a blessing. "*Labor omnia vincit improbus*," Trollope tells us in *Barchester Towers* (quoting Vergil), a formula he repeats in his *Autobiography*, in which his own dutiful devotion to labor, as we shall see, is chronicled in laborious detail. Yet this transformation from curse to blessing is enacted by precious few. The lesson of many novels in the last third of the nineteenth century is that labor leads to poverty. The conclusion of Butler's *The Way of All Flesh* is that labor is bad for you, wealth is good for you, and the former can never result in the latter. Ernest Pontifex, who declines from a clergyman (a profession in which one's labor is redeemed by respectability) to a shopkeeper and finally to a mender of old clothes, suddenly grows "brown and strong" again when he comes into an inherited fortune. On the other hand, Gissing's heroes seldom have such luck; the more they work, the poorer they become. The same transparently double attitude toward work expressed by Uriah Heep occurs often in Gissing. In *Eve's Ransom*, for example, Dengate tells Hilliard that he arrived at his present earning power of two pounds an hour (as opposed to Hilliard's two pounds a week) by "hard and honest work." But Hilliard later declares to Eve, "the devil take your work—for he alone is the originator of such accursed toil."

This bifurcation of attitudes toward work is a social bifurcation, of course. Those who don't have to work see it as a good—for those who do. In this chapter and the following, I will trace this uneasy suture of labor and leisure, first in the kind of novel that appears with increasing frequency toward the end of the century—the novel of working-class life—then in Henry James, whose men and women of leisure often turn

[1]Max Weber, *The Protestant Ethic and the Spirit of Capitalism*, trans. Talcott Parsons (New York: Scribner's, 1950), and R. H. Tawney, *Religion and the Rise of Capitalism* (New York: Harcourt, Brace, 1937).

out to be laborers in disguise. The distinction between novels of
work and the novels of James is often thought of as a distinction
between naturalism and high art, and to some degree this is
true. But James's high aesthetic mode, as we shall see, contains legible traces of the sordid world of poverty and work,
and not all novels about laborers were written by naturalists;
in fact, the masterpiece of such fiction, Knut Hamsun's *Hunger*, could also be thought of as the first modern text.

Factory novels—proletarian novels—occur throughout the
nineteenth century, in England going back as far as the 1830s
to Charlotte Elizabeth Tonna, author of *Helen Fleetwood* and
other "social problem" novels. Dickens of course, often wrote
about the working class—particularly in *Hard Times*—though,
according to James, "the case of Dickens was absolutely special; he dealt intensely with 'lower middle,' with 'lowest' middle, elements, but he escaped the predicament of showing
them as vulgar by showing them also as prodigiously droll.
When his people are not funny, who shall say what they
are?"[2] According to James, George Gissing shall say what
they are, an author for whom the master professes a "persistent taste."[3] To Gissing, we might add his lesser forerun-
ners and contemporaries: Elizabeth Gaskell, Disraeli, Charles
Kingsley, George Moore, Arthur Morrison, and, in America,
Jack London, Frank Norris, and Stephen Crane. Many of
these were shown the way, of course, by Zola and the French
naturalists. Even James himself wrote of the vulgar lowest
middle in *The Princess Casamassima*. Indeed, few novels of the
last two or three decades of the century were untouched by at
least a glance at what Disraeli called the "other nation," because the other nation was making itself visible. For this rea-

[2]Henry James, "London," *Harper's Weekly* 41 (31 July 1897):754. This
brief "letter" from London, of which James wrote a series, takes Gissing as
its main topic.
[3]Ibid.

son my choice of examples, before I turn to Gissing and Hamsun and eventually to James, will range across a broad spectrum of literary styles and will be guided initially by the appearance in fiction of the defining characteristic of the life of the "lowest middle": physical labor.

Attitudes toward labor usually vary according to the necessity it represents. Work is paradoxically most valuable and ennobling to those who are not forced to sell it. Thus, one of the most powerful descriptions of work in fiction occurs in *Anna Karenina*, the scene in which Levin spends a day mowing with his peasants. The scene is tinged with romance and nostalgia because of our radically different economic conditions today; an equivalent situation for us would have to take the form of parody, a liquor company president picking grapes with his Mexican employees, for example, something he would do only to invite newspaper coverage (like the college president who became a garbage collector for a year in order to write a book about it). Tolstoy carries the episode off, however, by concentrating on the power of the work itself, and on Levin's pride in responding to the unspoken challenge of his peasants. One of the insights of a vastly different novel, Zola's *Germinal*, is to perceive both qualities in the less romantic and more dangerous work of coal mining. As tedious, difficult, and inhuman as the work is, it gives Étienne and Maheu and their fellow workers a certain satisfaction that flows from the exertion of physical strength and from pride in knowing one's job and doing it well. Of course the workers realize that they are being exploited and that their wages are not even sufficient to feed their families. So the satisfaction is an alienated one, but still powerful enough that the men are able to lose themselves in their work every bit as much as Levin mowing his fields, or, say, as Ishmael squeezing whale sperm in *Moby Dick*.

These three examples—Levin mowing his fields, the descriptions of the whaling process in *Moby Dick*, and the accounts of coal mining in *Germinal*—show that work and narrative have a certain affinity for each other. A rhythm and pace take over the narrative that at least in part constitute the rhythm of work passing into the language. This is one of the oldest rhythms in storytelling, because it harkens back to the time Walter Benjamin talks about when storytelling and listening took place in conjunction with work such as weaving or spinning.[4] When Zola describes Étienne's first day in the mines, the manifest content of the narrative is his overpowering pain and fatigue. But behind and pervading this content is the slow, mesmerizing necessity of the work itself. The tedium of work becomes in the narrative a form of time stripped bare and proceeding at a uniform pace, not slowed down or speeded up or summarized for effect. Bits of information contribute to this pace as if they were parceling out and distributing the work over the long stretch of time it must occupy. They become like the coal the miners fill their tubs with:

> The four colliers had spread themselves out, one above the other, to cover the whole coal-face. Each one occupied about four metres of the seam, and there were hooked planks between them to catch the coal as it fell. The seam was so thin, hardly more than fifty centimetres through at this point, that they were flattened between roof and wall, dragging themselves along by their knees and elbows, unable to turn without grazing their shoulders. In order to get at the coal, they had to lie on one side with twisted neck, arms above their heads, and wield their short-handled picks slantways.
>
> Zacharie was at the bottom, with Levaque and Chaval above him and Maheu at the top. Each cut into the bed of shale with his pick, then made two vertical slots in the coal and finally drove an iron wedge in at the top, thus loosening a block. The coal was soft, and in its fall the block broke up and rolled in pieces all over the men's stomachs and thighs. When these

---

[4]Walter Benjamin, *Illuminations*, trans. Harry Zohn (New York: Schocken Books, 1969), p. 91.

pieces, stopped by the planks, had collected beneath them, the men disappeared, immured in the narrow cleft.[5]

A similar passage occurs in Norris's *McTeague*, when McTeague goes back to work in the gold mines in California. Norris's craft (like Zola's) was a kind of "carpentry," as Kenneth Rexroth puts it,[6] and in each writer we sense in the third-person, self-effacing narrative a form of work, of patient, slow construction. Work and narrative in these writers are continuous activities made up of discrete moments and pieces. In both, time refuses to mount, stretch, compress, or display depths; emptied of anticipation and memory, time becomes occupied entirely by material existence.

Zola goes one step further in *Germinal*, however. When its material base dissolves, time stops. That is, when the miners go on strike, they experience a parody of the leisure of the rich: empty time in which they may simply *be*, not *do*. But Zola insists that such leisure is far more deadly than the work the men have forgone. On strike, the miners sit around dreaming of money and pawn their few possessions for food. Their dream of money takes the childlike form of a treasure to be seized, no doubt because their only experience of money has been the parsimonious one of time parceled out by the conditions of labor. Even Étienne is in awe before capital, which is simply money freed of labor and time, and therefore a dream for those forced to work. As one of the capitalists, Deneulin, says, "The money other people earn for you is the best to get fat on." In this respect the anarchist Souvarine is correct when he exclaims with disgust that the workers' hatred for the bourgeoisie stems from their desire to be bourgeois themselves:

[5]The translation of *Germinal* is by Leonard Tancock (Harmondsworth: Penguin Books, 1978).
[6]Kenneth Rexroth, Afterword to the Signet Classic edition of *McTeague* (New York, 1964), p. 347.

"Can you understand this?" he asks Étienne. "A couple of hat-makers at Marseilles have drawn the lucky number in a lottery—a prize of a hundred thousand francs—and straight away they have invested it in annuities, saying they were never going to work any more! Yes, all you French workers have that one idea: you want to dig up a treasure and live on it for evermore in selfish and lazy isolation."

The culmination of the ironic leisure of the strike—in which some of the workers starve to death—is the riot, which itself becomes an ironic hallucination of work. Zola's description of the mobs rushing crazily over the countryside is surely one of the supreme achievements of naturalism, because his journalistic instincts serve him beautifully: he doesn't artificially inflate our excitement with rhetoric or excessive description, but simply follows the mob like a reporter. That is, his language follows instead of invents the natural surge and random collective misdirection of the crowd. With the tools of work—axes, files, and crowbars—the miners destroy the machines of work, the boilers, cables, and pumps at the pitheads. But they thereby succeed in destroying themselves rather than the capitalists, whom a recession has enabled to weather the strike. They chant, "We want bread!" as if all their blind activity had a goal, as if it really were work. But, as Zola makes clear, it is a grotesque parody of work, an orgy of work on a holiday, manic and incendiary as well as crazy and random—the very opposite of the linked, goal-oriented activities of labor. His point seems to be that the conditions of work for the miners impose this absolute split: either one is tied to time by the tedium of repeated operations—work—or one attempts to defeat time by a kind of crazy, destructive explosiveness. Only in the diabolical figure of Souvarine, who methodically saws through the timbers holding back an underground lake in the mine shaft, do the polarities of work and destruction come together.

Of the four great novels that deal with mining—*Germinal*, *McTeague*, *Nostromo*, and *Women in Love*—*Germinal* is perhaps the most journalistically accurate. But the greatest is undoubtedly *Nostromo*. Curiously enough, we never see men at work in Conrad's novel. There are no passages in *Nostromo* like the one quoted above from *Germinal*, in which labor and narrative find a common rhythm. Instead, released from the necessity of process, Conrad's prose for the first third of the novel spirals and hovers in a self-sustaining gesture that is one of the first dazzling performances of literary modernism. Critics like Albert Guerard who see the latter half of *Nostromo* as a performance of a more tepid, conventional nature—a reversion to mere nineteenth-century realism—have missed the linked series of transformations the novel enacts. The Monterist revolution in Sulaco displaces the silver of the mine from its normal round of circulation and makes it (spirited away in a boat by Nostromo and Decoud) a form of plunder, a treasure. Conrad's panoramic method allows us to witness money undergoing a process of devolution, from Holroyd's distant capital to processed silver to treasure buried in the earth. Repeatedly, the narrative pushes not forward, but backward, fueled by the nearly instinctual nostalgia of the characters, their need to recover what they think they have lost in order to survive. And the push backward occurs formally as well as temporally; just as the enormous historical realities of capital and labor that made the mine profitable give way to the imagination of power, to historical romance, and finally to the image of a treasure (something illicit, released from work), so the narrative devolves from historical panorama to fable. *Nostromo* is a historical panorama deconstructing itself "in a revulsion of subjectiveness," to use a phrase Conrad applied to his central character. As the characters diminish, as their limits become increasingly prescribed by monadic darkness, forests, ocean, or fog as well as by the absurdities of South American politics, so that they feel "the crushing, paralyzing sense of human littleness," they also turn inward in order to feast upon their private fantasies, for the most part fantasies of power and wealth.

But a final transformation takes place beyond this, one that links *Nostromo* firmly to the novels of labor under discussion here. It occurs when Nostromo decides he must grow rich very slowly. With this resolution, which entails digging up the treasure a little at a time in order to avoid suspicion, the novel reverts from fable to ordinary reality. Ordinary reality is not social reality, but the reality of isolated individuals in a material world, the kind of reality we find ourselves on the verge of at the end of Dostoevsky's *The Gambler:* a reality of small daily increments, of living each minute methodically and with prudence, of growing rich or growing poor very slowly, bit by bit. In other words, the reality of labor. The treasure in this case is no longer a treasure, for the same reason that Alexis in *The Gambler* will never again win a fortune: because money has become a finite limit, an exhaustible bank account. Money is something one chips away at little by little, and though we never witness Nostromo on the night shift digging up his plunder (just as we never witness the miners in the silver mine), it is evident by the novel's end that he has become a slave to work, like Dostoevsky's Alexis. In both novels, money comes full circle; produced by labor that has been purchased by capital, it accumulates in pools, transforms itself into treasure, then completes the arc in the piecemeal form of payment for labor once more.

As Edward Said points out, most of the characters in *Nostromo* are eager to leave records of their thoughts and actions.[7] Of the two extensive written records, Decoud's letters and Don José Avellanos's book, Decoud's becomes part of the text of *Nostromo*. Said also traces Conrad's own record of the act of composing *Nostromo*, an act the author repeatedly compared to exhausting physical labor: "Formerly in my sea life, a difficulty nerved me to the effort: now I perceive it is not so. . . . I say so because for me, writing—the only possible writing—is just simply the conversion of nervous force

[7]Edward Said, *Beginnings* (New York: Basic Books, 1975), p. 100.

into phrases."[8] We sense Conrad mining his materials, squeezing himself into smaller and smaller spaces, like the coal miners in *Germinal*, until "it is like being in a tomb which is at the same time a hell where one must write, write, write."[9] If the work per se occurs offstage in *Nostromo*—if we never see the miners mining or Nostromo digging—it may very well be because such work is incapable of leaving a record: it is neither (in Said's terms) action not thought, or, rather, it is action and thought appropriated by external economic forces. Conrad's labor in writing *Nostromo*, on the other hand, was painful to him precisely because of its isolation, its unreciprocated effort. It was physical labor deprived of physical means and physical issue, a self-generating product that neither improved the yield of nature nor entertained those engaged in such improvement. In other words, it was neither quite useful nor entirely useless, neither ingenious labor nor the product of leisure.

I borrow some of my terms in this discussion from Kurt Heinzelman's analysis of attitudes toward labor in the eighteenth and nineteenth centuries. The only good labor, according to Adam Smith (in Heinzelman's account) is that which produces ecnomically useful commodities. In answer to this, William Morris asserted that alienated labor is not productive of moral or cultural good; only handicrafts are—by implication, art.[10] To this absolute split of labor and art corresponds the split we are beginning to trace in these two chapters, between labor and leisure, as well as between the art of work and the work of art. Conrad's novel is riven by this split; it is a historical novel whose subject is subjectivity, written in a mimetic language that is also self-generating. There is nothing

[8]Letter to H. G. Wells, quoted in Said, *Beginnings*, p. 102.

[9]Letter to A. H. Davray, ibid.

[10]Kurt Heinzelman, *The Economics of the Imagination* (Amherst: University of Massachusetts Press, 1980), pp. 153–157. Here I have simplified a complex argument; the interested reader may look at the entire chapter, "The Art of Labor," in Heinzelman's book.

quite like it in either the realist or the modernist tradition, but if it stands outside these two traditions it also stands equally high.

The degree to which writers toward the end of the nineteenth century were becoming conscious of the split between labor and art may be seen in the increasing frequency with which journalists appear in novels, those laborers of the written word. They appear earlier in the century too—in quite a few of Trollope's novels, in Dickens's *Bleak House*, and in Balzac's *Illusions perdues*. But by the end of the century their ranks have multiplied. There is Bartley Hubbard in Howells's novels, Henrietta Stackpole in *The Portrait of a Lady*, the unnamed narrator of Hamsun's *Hunger*, Decoud in *Nostromo*, Merton Densher in *The Wings of the Dove*, Jasper Milvain and several other characters in Gissing's *New Grub Street*. We cannot help thinking of Zola as a kind of journalist too, dressed in his black frock coat and hard hat taking notes in a mine while the colliers labored before him. Most naturalism, following Zola's lead, has a journeymanlike quality not unlike that we associate with newspaper writing. The style of pure information is actually one of the more powerful styles available to fiction, and it displays the intimacy with journalism that fiction has always possessed.

But the presence of so many journalists in novels of this period, and the tendency of certain novelists to write journalistically, suggests other possibilities too. We know that newspapers and journals were mushrooming in the second half of the nineteenth century, that journalism as a trade attracted more and more of the educated middle class, that more people could read and wanted material to read, even (or especially) if it was only "good, coarse, marketable stuff for the world's vulgar," as Jasper Milvain says in *New Grub Street*. As early as Balzac, we see potentially serious writers portrayed in fiction as corrupted by journalism, cheapened by the necessity to make a buck. As Lukács puts it, *Illusions perdue* portrays journalism as a form of alientated labor, "the transformation of literature into a commodity."[11] This is a familiar theme in Marxist criticism, and it surfaces often in novels of the time. Again, from *New Grub Street:* "Literature nowadays is a trade. . . . Your successful man of letters is your skillful tradesman. He thinks first and foremost of the market; when one kind of goods begins to go off slackly, he is ready with something new and appetising." And the narrator of *Hunger* weighs a piece of writing in his hand and assesses it on the spot "with a rough guess as five kroner."

This fascination with writing as labor and with the written text as marketable commodity may be familiar, but it still doesn't fail to make us uncomfortable. We prefer to associate novels with leisure, the leisure to write and the leisure to read. We do not like to think that good writers have to earn money, or that the conditions under which they earn it are determined by the economic system in which they live. We appreciate it rather when they starve or grub for food, as Henry Miller did in Paris. Thus, when Trollope revealed in his autobiography that he wrote a predetermined number of words per day and pages per week, his literary stock immediately went down.

Trollope's *An Autobiography* was published in 1883, after his death, only five years before Gissing began *New Grub Street*, which may well have been inspired by Trollope's example. In it Trollope refers to one of his novels explicitly as a "marketable commodity,"[12] and he has this to say about the "profession" of novelist: "I confess that my first object in taking to literature as a profession was that which is common to the barrister when he goes to the Bar, and to the baker when he sets up his oven. I wished to make an income on which I and those belonging to me might live in comfort."[13] Trollope

[11]Georg Lukács, *Studies in European Realism* (New York: Grosset and Dunlap, 1964), p. 49.

[12]Anthony Trollope, *An Autobiography* (London: Oxford University Press, 1950), p. 109.

[13]Ibid., pp. 107–108. Compare Mr. Henry Gowan, the painter, in

writes somewhat facetiously when he juxtaposes these three "professions." He knew very well that only four professions were respectable in his time (in descending order): the clergy, the military, the law, and medicine. That is, gentlemen might practice these professions and still remain gentlemen. Mrs. Clay's long speech about the advantages and disadvantages of the various professions in *Persuasion* grudgingly grants honor to these four, though she prefers "the lot of those who are not obliged to follow any [profession], who can live in a regular way, in the country, choosing their own hours." Lady Amelia in Trollope's *Doctor Thorne*, on the other hand, declares that a woman of blood may not marry any man who earns his bread, and she lumps doctors and lawyers in with butchers, though she herself winds up married to a lawyer. The very concept of a "profession," it becomes clear in the nineteenth century, in what used to be a hereditary, customary, and neofeudal society is an accommodation for capitalism and a money economy. Second-born sons and impoverished nobles cannot be expected to go to the workhouse; therefore, with clearly marked divisions between the middle class and the nobility, a kind of hybrid gentleman appears, one whose labor can be seen as a polite public service that also happens to be remunerative.

But one more "profession" became somewhat honorable during the century, though its status was always uncertain, ambiguous: that of the artist, in particular the writer. *An Autobiography* is Trollope's bid to establish it firmly as a profession, a part of the venerable list (repeated several times) of callings "in law, in physic, in religious teaching, in art, or literature."[14] To do this, he belittles inspiration and insists that writing novels requires little more than application:

Dickens's *Little Dorrit:* "What I do in my trade, I do to sell. What all we fellows do, we do to sell. If we didn't want to sell it for the most we can get for it, we shouldn't do it. Being work, it has to be done."

[14]Trollope, *Autobiography*, p. 106.

I have allotted myself so many pages a week. The average number has been about 40. It has been placed as low as 20, and has risen to 112. And as a page is an ambiguous term, my page has been made to contain 250 words; and as words, if not watched, will have a tendency to straggle, I have had every word counted as I went. In the bargains I have made with publishers I have,—not, of course, with their knowledge, but in my own mind,—undertaken always to supply them with so many words, and I have never put a book out of hand short of the number by a single word.[15]

This well-known passage still startles us today with its strange combination of honesty and boastful umbleness. Trollope may very well have thought that the doors of great houses would never open to writers if they behaved at all idiosyncratically, or if their labor were a form of spiritual torment as it was for Conrad thirty years later. Better to think of writing as no more aberrant than clerking: "I therefore venture to advise young men who look forward to authorship as the business of their lives, even when they propose that that authorship be of the highest class known, to avoid enthusiastic rushes with their pens, and to seat themselves at their desks day by day as though they were lawyers' clerks;—and so let them sit till the allotted task shall be accomplished."[16] Repeatedly he refers to writing as work or labor and to the writer as a workman, and it becomes clear in these references that his attitude toward work consisted of that fortunate median the protestant West discovered (or created) between work as a curse and work as a blessing: work was a duty.

Trollope's attitudes find a grotesque reflection in Gissing's *New Grub Street*. "I tell you," Milvain says, "writing is a business. Get together half a dozen specimens of the Sunday-school prize; study them; discover the essential points of such composition; hit upon new attractions; then go to work me-thodically, so many pages a day." The echo here of Trollope's *Autobiography* is unmistakable, as it is in this account of Edwin Reardon's labor to finish his novel:

> After all, there came a day when Edwin Reardon found himself regularly at work once more, ticking off his stipulated quantum of manuscript each four-and-twenty hours. He wrote a very small hand; sixty written slips of the kind of paper he habitually used would represent . . . a passable three-hun-dred-page volume. On an average he could write four such slips a day; so here we have fifteen days for the volume, and forty-five for the completed book.

Of course for Reardon this process is a form of torture, not duty, and it eventually kills him. Repeatedly in *New Grub Street*, writers are portrayed as laborers whose work warps them physically. Alfred Yule walks with his eyes fixed on the ground, like Lawrence's colliers in *Women in Love*. His shoulders are bent, his body cramped. "He could do nothing light-handedly. He seemed always to converse with effort; he took a seat with stiff ungainliness; he walked with a stumbling or sprawling gait." His daughter Marian speculates that sooner or later someone will invent a literary machine: "Only to throw in a given number of old books, and have them re-duced, blended, modernised into a single one for today's con-sumption." Indeed, a persistent theme in *New Grub Street* is that writing is a form of material production that exacts a material toll. Gissing dwells upon the various material condi-tions surrounding the production of a novel, from the privacy or lack of privacy in Edwin Reardon's three rooms (a theme echoed in *The Nether World*, *The Way of All Flesh*, *The Wings of the Dove*, and Virginia Woolf's *A Room of One's Own*) to the toil of writing itself, to the paper industry that makes book pro-duction possible, to the market forces that determine how much an author will be paid, what he should write about, and how long his novels should be. Three-volume novels, we learn in *New Grub Street*, are going out of favor. Whelpdale's "Novel-writing taught in ten lessons" advises novelists "to write of the wealthy middle class." In an echo of Balzac's *Illusions perdues*, Jasper Milvain declares that "if that article [paper] were not so cheap and so abundant, people wouldn't have so much temptation to scribble." One of the characters at the novel's edge, John Yule, begins his professional career as a bookseller, then works for a newspaper, and finally makes his fortune in paper manufacture. One senses in this sequence a careful regression from literature to cheap paper to raw material.

Of course the point is that, once they are considered marketable commodities, novels are no less and no more material than, say, boots. Leaking up between the cracks of the social world in *New Grub Street*—and in most of Gissing's novels—this material world repeatedly insists upon its presence and priority. Would Gissing have been consoled by contemporary critical theorists who perceive in a text an infinite regression of other texts that bracket out the material world? No doubt he would have seen right through them. But the problem of *New Grub Street* is the problem one of its characters, Harold Biffen, faces: how to represent in fiction a truly material reality, the kind that is unredeemed—indeed, untouched—by the romance of most novels, as well as by idealist conceptions of language. Gissing does it at least in part by making the reader aware of the book in his hand: its weight and price, its physical presence. If a book is an object, so is a novel: the manuscript can be sold to a publisher, and the printed book can be pawned. In *New Grub Street* we learn that all objects are convertible, can be exchanged for each other by virtue of their homogeneous materiality. But in the process of exchange they wear down, they lose value. The pawnshop plays an important role in *New Grub Street*, as it does in *The Nether World* and in Norris's *McTeague*, Dostoevsky's *Crime and Punishment*, Zola's *L'assommoir* and *Germinal*, and (as we shall see) Hamsun's *Hunger*. In pawning, a kind of second law of thermodynamics applies: something is always lost in the transaction. One receives less and less money for more and more things. And like coins passed from hand to hand, the things themselves become worn in the process. Furniture takes on the look of used furniture, clothes no longer fit. Commodities diminish in this parody of exchange, become worn in the social flow that milks them of value, until they finally break down entirely. The pawnbroker's shelves are only a halfway house in this process, a temporary resting place, their organization minimal and purely external. Eventually things pass over from a state of being garments and books and furniture to being cloth and paper and wood. In *New Grub Street* the final stage is never quite reached, though we sense its imminence in the physical object in our hands, the book. For the most part Gissing portrays intermediate stages: "His necktie was discoloured and worn. Coat and waistcoat might pass muster, but of the trousers the less said the better. One of his boots was patched, and both were all but heelless." A characteristic device in Gissing is to list a sequence of objects, as though each one represented a degenerative stage of the one before: "His score of volumes must rank upon the mantelpiece; his clothing must be kept in the trunk. Cups, plates, knives, forks and spoons would lie in the little open cupboard, the lowest section of which was for his supply of coals." One senses in such passages a literal material flow, a causal chain. The same sort of thing occurs on a larger scale in *The Nether World*: "The sky hung low and murky, or, rather, was itself invisible, veiled by the fume of factory chimneys; a wailing wind rattled the sash and the door. A newly lighted fire refused to flame cheerfully, half smothered in its own smoke, which every now and then was blown downwards and out into the room."

We might expect that in *New Grub Street* Harold Biffen's ambition to write a novel that would treat "ordinary vulgar life with fidelity and seriousness" was also Gissing's; but it was not. Gissing portrays Biffen with affectionate humor before killing him off and makes his project in fact sound like the impossible thing it is: "I want to deal with the essentially unheroic, with the day-to-day life of that vast majority of people who are at the mercy of paltry circumstances. . . . The result will be something unutterably tedious. Precisely. That is the stamp of the ignobly decent life." When Reardon suggests that "there may surely exist such a thing as the *art* of fiction," Biffen replies, "it is worked out." Even Zola, he insists, writes "deliberate tragedies," whose lowest figures "become heroic from the place they will fill in a strongly imagined drama." Biffen wants to write of a life that is entirely unredeemed by the sort of dramatic scenes that occur in novels, a life in which fictional time becomes identical to ordinary time and nothing is shaped or cut out. And he wants, "among other things, to insist upon the fateful power of trivial incidents. No one has yet dared to do this seriously. It has often been done in farce, and that's why farcical writing so often makes one melancholy." There would be no consoling humor in Biffen's novel as there is, say, when Dickens portrays common life.

Biffen sounds like Henry James describing what was Gissing's genius: to portray vulgar people without making them funny. Following the passage quoted at this chapter's beginning, in which James points out that Dickens's "lowest middle" characters are always "droll," he declares that Gissing, on the other hand, "*is* serious—almost imperturbably—about them, and, as it turns out, even quite manfully and admirably sad. He has the great thing: his saturation (with the visible and audible common) can project itself, let him get outside and walk round it." But then James strikes a note very different from Biffen's: "I scarcely think he stays, as it were, outside quite as much as he might; and on the question of form he certainly strikes me as staying far too little."[17] We can translate this into a complaint that Gissing lacked James's preoc-

[17]James, "London," p. 754.

cupation with the distancing effect of aesthetic form. But in fact, for the most part Gissing was a formalist. He couldn't write the novel Biffen finally wrote, *Mr. Bailey, Grocer*, except as a subtext literally unopened in *New Grub Street*. Gissing's plots and scenes, his dramatic action, his selection of events are all conventional. At the same time, he acknowledges through his character Biffen the need to find a new form, one whose relative formlessness would be more appropriate to the task of representing ordinary reality, the kind of reality novels like *Nostromo* and *The Gambler* bring us to the verge of.

But the question remains: Can it be done? The reviews of Biffen's book quoted in *New Grub Street* suggest that he turned out to be merely another naturalist. The problem with naturalism is that the trivial and the random—signs of ordinary reality—become absorbed by a programmatic necessity. Whether Biffen fell into the Darwinian simplicities of Zola, Norris, and occasionally Gissing we will never know, but we can perhaps safely assume that his ordinary reality was not ordinary enough. Do we watch Mr. Bailey, grocer, stocking his shelves, making change, sitting in his chair, saying nothing, sleeping? The ordinary reality of work is a reality of slow accumulation in which nothing is accumulated. It can't enter fiction without dragging its shadow, the anarchic, the violent, and the random. The year before *New Grub Street* was published, Gissing's contemporary Knut Hamsun published a novel in Norway of which English novelists would be ignorant for nearly half a century. The two men were writing their novels at exactly the same time. Like *New Grub Street*, *Hunger* deals with the poverty of a writer forced to market his writings as commodities, a writer whose need for food repeatedly drives him to the pawnshop until he has nothing left to pawn. But unlike *New Grub Street*—and unlike *Mr. Bailey, Grocer*— *Hunger* uncovers the secret of representing ordinary reality in fiction. The secret is that ordinary reality, conceived of as the reality of both labor and unemployment, the reality of the low and of the vulgar, of poverty, is neither ordinary nor real. Rather, it is a hallucination.

As we have seen in *The Gambler* and in *Germinal*, a good narrative is a form of work that at certain intervals swings toward a reality the opposite of work: play, chance, anarchy, violence. Hamsun's *Hunger* intensifies this process by alternating accounts of trivial daily events and domestic details with hallucinatory, desperate random activities such as shouting a meaningless word in someone's face on the street or knocking on an arbitrary door and making up a story on the spot. Eventually everything becomes permeated by the hallucinatory, which is nothing more than the ordinary under the spell of the random and discrete, the world in pieces with each piece seen in grotesque close-up:

> I was aware of every detail of what was going on around me. A big brown dog ran across the street, toward the trees and the Tivoli; it had a small collar made of Mexican silver. Farther up the street, a window on the first story opened and a girl with her sleeves rolled up leaned out and began polishing the panes on the outside. Nothing escaped my eyes, I was sharp and my brain was very much alive, everything poured in toward me with a staggering distinctness as if a strong light had fallen on everything around me. The women before me had two blue feathers in their hats, and plaid kerchiefs around their necks.[18]

This is Flaubert beneath the magnifying glass of hysteria. The strong light that falls on everything in *Hunger* is the mental equivalent of an empty stomach, and it gives objects and events the paradoxical quality of the obsessive on the one hand and the contingent and common on the other.

[18]The translation of *Hunger* is by Robert Bly (New York: Farrar, Straus and Giroux, 1967).

Money and Fiction

The hunger of the title is a literal, material hunger; it is not a metaphor. It is a transitive need forced to take on the character of an intransitive desire, forced to become manic and distended, to take everything in. When the novel opens, the narrator hasn't eaten for several days. "I was becoming more and more nervous and irritable, and several mornings lately I had been so dizzy I had had to stay in bed all day." He has already pawned all his possessions for food. "I was so utterly denuded of objects that I didn't even have a comb left, or a book to read when I felt hopeless." But he does have pencil and paper. He stays alive by selling the newspapers articles on "Crimes of the Future" or "Freedom of the Will," though most of what he writes is rejected. Besides, what he really wants to write is something vaster, more ambitious: an investigation of philosophical consciousness in three volumes. But he can't; he's lost his pencil. The pencil was in the pocket of the waistcoat he pawned on an impulse to give some money to a beggar. By the time he retrieves it, he is unable to write. "Everything bothered me and distracted me; everything I saw obsessed me." He follows some girls on the street and tells one she is dropping her book, though she has no book. He wanders through the city with no purpose in mind. "I stopped at a corner without needing to, turned and went up small alleys without having anything to do there." He sits on a park bench and constructs a fantastic tissue of lies for an old man sitting beside him, an improbable narrative that mushrooms out of trivial small talk. He applies for a job but dates his letter 1848 (forty years earlier), wakes up the next morning and as though possessed writes feverishly fifteen, twenty pages of an article for a newspaper. He walks around with a borrowed blanket, sleeps in the woods, gets up at three the following afternoon and wanders back into town, weak, "throwing up here and there on the sly." On a whim, he rushes to the third floor of a building, rings a bell, and, when a woman answers, says: "I do beg your pardon, madam, for having rung so loud. I wasn't familiar with your bell. I believe that there is an invalid gen-

162

tleman here who has advertised for a man to give him outings in a chair?" He tries to exchange some barber coupons and a tie for money, but the banker he offers them to doesn't want them. He has already been thrown out of his room by his landlady, but with no place to go he sneaks back in and finds a letter from the newspaper editor to whom he had submitted his hastily written article, which has been accepted for ten kroner (about ten dollars). "I laughed and cried and ran down the street, stopped and beat my legs, swore wholesale at no one about nothing. And time went by. The whole night until dawn I went yodeling around the streets, dumfounded with joy, and said over and over: shows real ability, actually a little masterpiece, a stroke of genius. And ten kroner!"

So ends part 1 of *Hunger*. At the beginning of part 2, the narrator again has eaten nothing for two or three days, and the cycle of his hungry existence begins all over again. Part 3 is similar. It should be clear from this summary that this is a narrative unlike anything else in nineteenth-century fiction, with the possible exception of Dostoevsky's *Notes from Underground* or even *The Gambler*. Like Alexis in *The Gambler*, the narrator of *Hunger* submits himself to chance, but chance for him is not the thrill of risk; it is the desperation of whim. With the exception of the sale of his article, any money he obtains comes by chance: he meets a friend on the street and borrows five kroner; a grocer gives him someone else's change by mistake; a ten-kroner note arrives anonymously in an envelope. Money is never a reward for effort, for labor; the article he writes is a product not of the application Trollope praised, but of the inspiration he cautioned writers to avoid. Work is a linked series of operations, performed with deliberation and measure. In a capitalist world, to work in spurts is not to work at all, is to violate the predictable patterns work must fall into. Similarly, most realistic novels are linked series of events that fall into a pattern. But not *Hunger*. Few events lead to another, no patterns emerge, nothing has an issue. The novel is an unlinked series of crises, not a chain of complications leading to a climax. It ends as suddenly as it begins, when the narrator abruptly decides to take a job on a Swedish ship bound for England.

One of the newspaper articles the narrator thinks about writing will be called "The Freedom of the Will." In a certain respect this is ironic. Certainly no narrative written before *Hunger* (and few since it) possesses such freedom, let alone such desperate energy; but that freedom is a compulsive one, inseparable from the necessity of hunger. The hungry man is a kind of gambler in reverse, his will rendered impotent not by the restraints of mathematical necessity (as in *The Gambler*), but by a paradoxical lack of restraint, or of reciprocity. His hunger places him outside all social norms and expectations, gives him an empty space to wander in. In a sense this empty space is money, but money that is always somewhere else and thus makes its power felt by its absence. The narrator of *Hunger* attempts to do the impossible, to live without money. He needs money desperately, but when he gets it he often gives it away, just as upon eating a meal after three days of starving he throws it all up. In Henry James money often equals freedom, the freedom of Isabel Archer, for example, to soar above the commonplace, though such freedom turns out to be bondage in disguise. The reverse is true in *Hunger*. For Hamsun, the lack of money is a kind of bondage that produces a distorted, crazy, anarchic freedom, a freedom prankish, desperate, whimsical, and without memory. Freedom is innocence, money is shame. The narrator of *Hunger* possesses a fastidious sense of honor that prevents him from stealing anything even while starving and that torments him when a grocer mistakenly gives him someone else's change. He cannot keep the money; he gives it away to a cake seller. In a passage the exact reverse of that in Defoe's *Colonel Jack*, in which Jack becomes a man by buying pants with pockets to put his stolen money in, the narrator of *Hunger*, having rid himself of this shameful money, declares: "How wonderful it felt to be an honorable man again! My empty pockets no longer weighed me down, it was a delight to be broke again." In *Hunger*, money is manna. It comes from nowhere and disappears just as quickly. It is an inscrutable quasi-religious power, something outside the narrator's experience, something that possesses its own will. In one scene, while sitting on a park bench, he makes a cone from a sheet of paper and imagines it full of money:

> Hunger was beginning to attack me now. I sat staring at the white paper cornucopia, which looked as though swollen by silver coins, and I egged myself on to believe that it really did contain something . . . . I imagined the small, exquisite ten-øre coins at the bottom, and the flat, fluted krone pieces on top—a whole paper cone full of money.

Traditionally, cornucopias are imagined as pouring out not money, but goods, especially produce. This transformation of things into money or, more precisely, of the lack of things into the lack of money, is echoed throughout the novel. "I counted up my money once more: one half a pocket-knife, one key chain, but not an øre." We sense in *Hunger* that money has disappeared into the material flow of things and in doing so has become a kind of decoy money, a cipher, dumb and unserviceable. In one of the most startling and poignant little gestures in the novel, the narrator slices the buttons off his jacket and attempts to pawn them. These buttons, which he carries around in his pocket like coins after the pawnbroker refuses them, become a dumb money, like the word he invents in his delirium that can mean anything and so means nothing and is worthless.

The novel is filled with substitutes like these buttons. Instead of food, he chews on (at various times) a sliver of wood, a shaving, an old orange peel, a stone, and a patch of cloth from his pocket. To satisfy his hunger he swallows his spit over and over again, and "it did some good." Chewing on the sliver of wood, however, he says, "my teeth were tired of their fruitless labor, and I let them rest." Fruitless labor is a key to *Hunger*. "Hadn't I applied for jobs, and listened to lectures, and written articles, and read and worked night and day like a madman?" Behind *Hunger* lies an assumption central to the protestant, bourgeois West, that to be genuine work must be an activity that cannot be enjoyed. To punish himself on his fourth day without food, he *makes* himself run down the street, then makes himself sit in uncomfortable places. If he can't have labor, he must have its effects, physical discomfort and exhaustion. Then at least he will have *something;* something will have resulted from an expenditure of effort. Nothing is more frightening than to will or perform an act with no result—to, for example, open his mouth and laugh and laugh and realize that not a sound is coming out.

On the other hand—as if to compensate for this fruitless labor—the novel is also filled with images of production out of nothing, of which the paper cornucopia is the most obvious example. Staring at it, he hears a policeman cough, so he coughs too. "Now, won't he jump for that paper cone when he comes near? I sat rejoicing over this joke, I rubbed my hands in ecstasy and swore magnificently. . . . I had become intoxicated with starvation, my hunger had made me drunk." To become drunk on hunger is to become drunk on nothing— hunger itself is a cornucopia, the production of something out of nothing. He writes his best articles on an empty stomach and an empty head; he constructs romances, dreams of Princess Ylayali out of the same emptiness, and he tells fantastic lies to strangers on the street. In one of the novel's most memorable passages, he invents out of nothing—plucks out of the air—a brand new word, *kuboaa:*

> I had arrived at the joyful insanity hunger was: I was empty
> and free of pain, and my thoughts no longer had any check. I
> debated everything silently with myself. My thoughts took
> amazing leaps as I tried to establish the meaning of my new

word. It needn't mean either *God* or *Tivoli Gardens,* and who
said it had to mean *cattle show?* I clenched my fists hard and
repeated: who said it had to mean *cattle show?* When I thought
it over, it was in fact not even necessary that it mean *padlock* or
sunrise. In a word like that it was very easy to find meaning.

Like the buttons in his pocket, which are not money, or the
paper cornucopia that does not contain money, *kuboaa* at least
possesses the trace of a material existence, at least it is something, a sound, though it means nothing. It is like a coin
whose face is worn; it promises much but is curiously inert.
The production of something out of nothing, however, has
this danger, that even the something will evaporate. The more
he thinks about his "remarkable word," the more his thoughts
fly off into spiraling orbits: "I had formulated my opinion on
what the word did not mean, but I had not yet come to a
decision on what it *did* mean. 'That is a secondary matter!' I
said aloud to myself, and grabbed myself by the arm and
repeated that it was a secondary matter. . . . It occurred to me
that someone was talking, butting into my chat, and I answered angrily: 'I beg your pardon? For an idiot, you are all
alone in the field! *Yarn?* Go to hell!' Why should I be obligated to let it mean *yarn* when I had a special aversion to its
meaning *yarn?*" And so forth. We cannot fail to see in all this a
hallucinatory version of the writer's job—the production of
words—as well as of the capitalist's production of something
out of nothing, of more money out of less.

Kuboaa in a sense *is* the novel *Hunger:* a text produced out of
emptiness. We think of novels as the product—paradoxically—of leisure. This one is the product of an ironic leisure
enforced by the necessity of hunger, which literally is the
nothing that is something, the absence in the stomach that
creates delirium. The hungry man invents his word *kuboaa*
while in a prison cell reserved for respectable people who have
lost their keys and cannot return to their flats. "But I was, of
course, in the reserved section, high above the prisoners. A

homeless cabinet minister, if I may be so bold." Sprinkled throughout the novel are similar ironic references to the life of leisure. "Would you be interested in a walk down to the pier? I said to myself. I mean, only, of course, if you can spare the time?" Like the miners on strike in *Germinal*, the narrator of *Hunger* has no employment; he is a man of leisure in the most literal sense, one who does not work. Instinctively, he knows that in the eyes of those he meets the only difference between being taken for a true man of leisure—one who does not *have* to work—and a pauper lies in appearances. So he struts before old friends on the street like a wealthy gentleman and lies to them about his life. At times he even seems to shun the very money he needs, as though money were beneath his consideration.

His sits in his room and takes careful note of his surroundings, like a gentleman with all the time in the world, like one of James's protagonists, for whom the world has become a matter of attentive observation. In James, observant men of leisure compose paintings out of their surroundings. Here is the Prince Casamassima, in the novel named for his wife, gazing out a window:

> The aspect of South Street, Mayfair, on a Sunday afternoon in August, is not enlivening, yet the Prince had stood for ten minutes gazing out of the window at the genteel vacancy of the scene; at the closed blinds of the opposite houses, the lonely policeman on the corner, covering a yawn with a white cotton hand, the low-pitched light itself, which seemed conscious of an obligation to observe the decency of the British Sabbath. Our personage, however, had a talent for that kind of attitude; it was one of the things by which he had exasperated his wife; he could remain motionless, with the aid of some casual support for his high, lean person, considering serenely and inexpressively any object that might lie before him and presenting his aristocratic head at a favorable angle, for periods of extraordinary length.

Similar scenes occur in *The Ambassadors;* Strether creates impressionist paintings wherever he goes. What is art, asks the Princess Casamassima, "but a synthesis made in the interest of pleasure?" *Hunger* begins with the narrator looking out his window, in what sounds like a parody of the aristocratic leisure of the Prince in the passage above. The things he sees, however, refuse to become a synthesis. If James is an impressionist, Hamsun prefigures the collages done by the dadaists and surrealists in the 1920s. Under the spell of even the calmest hysteria, the physical world refuses to organize, to become anything but de trop, inert:

> I opened the window and looked out. I could see a clothesline and an open field. Behind them there was some debris from a burned-down blacksmith's shop which the workmen were just now clearing away. Leaning my elbows on the windowsill, I gazed up into the sky. Today would be clear. The fall had come, that cool and delicious time of the year when everything changed color and died.

This is in fact one of the most subdued passages in the novel (perhaps because it appears on the second page), but its relative calm enables us to sense what a profoundly different character the material world had for Hamsun than for any other nineteenth-century novelist. The separate objects observed here are not linked, but simply juxtaposed. Nothing is symbolic or metaphoric unless it be the debris from the blacksmith's shop, since everything seen here has the quality of debris, of fragments, of unrelated pieces of the material world. The clothesline, the field, the debris, the sky are random bits of matter, unorganized and dead; but their death is not splendid or beautiful or tragic or horrible—it is merely a matter of fact: "everything changed color and died." The significance of this landscape is that it has no significance. We have come a long way from Jane Austen, but we can see quite clearly the effect of Mr. Elliot's hammer.

The ordinary world here *is* ordinary. But surely there must be something else? The impulse to read the world as a text, to interpret its signs, cannot be shaken off by the narrator of *Hunger*. In his delirium, the most trivial things and events appear large and consequential. When an old man sits beside him on a park bench carrying an outdated newspaper, he decides it must be a rare number, maybe the only one of its kind. "Perhaps it was hiding official papers, dangerous documents stolen from some files. I had the vague impression of the existence of some secret treaty, a plot." But of course the paper is merely a paper, wrapped around the old man's meager lunch. In *Hunger*, large and consequential things are cut off from meaning, and trivial things are obsessive, threatening. Everything that happens to Hamsun's narrator—he bumps into someone on the street, his eyes fall on the words of an advertisement or on a woman's red scarf—happens with the double status of the necessary and the arbitrary. "Even in my highly worked-up state, I never lost for a moment my presence of mind. We drove past a policeman, and I took note that his badge was number 69. This figure struck me as gruesomely exact, in an instant it was driven like a sliver into my brain. 69, precisely 69, I would never forget that!" We may presume that Harold Biffen's mistake in *Mr. Bailey, Grocer* is his failure to perceive that the ordinary is "gruesomely exact." The ordinary is cut off from convention and history; it consists of objects and events that are simultaneously magnified and shrunken by the unmediated collision of the material and the subjective. Thus Hamsun is very much Kafka's precursor. When the narrator of *Hunger* marches with determination to the third floor of an apartment building and knocks on a door, we can't help but think of Joseph K. in *The Trial* wandering into a tenement, climbing the stairs, knocking on a door, and being admitted, as though by the most everyday miracle, to the law courts. This conjunction of chance and necessity—everything happens by chance, nothing happens by chance—which works its way loose from the scaffolding of plot so that it passes into the very existence of objects and events, is in many respects the beginning of that strain of the modern novel that runs from Kafka through Sartre to Beckett.

None of this would be true if *Hunger* were a novel of manners. Hamsun's novel shows us that when fiction loses the social theme, when its subject is not the relationship between the individual and society but the individual in isolation, then its structure undergoes a fundamental change. Things weave together in James; in Hamsun they unravel. One event doesn't necessarily lead to or result from or echo or contrast with another; events occur in a flat plane, a continuous possibility of events. It is only a short step from this sense of things to a view that the chief event in such a string of possibilities is the act of writing itself. Thus *Hunger* leads (not chronologically, of course) through Kafka and Henry Miller to Joyce and Beckett and the literature of exhaustion (a more polite form of hunger). In the midst of all this, incidently, money loses its importance. In the twentieth century we might say that money is so present it has become invisible, it has disappeared into the social and material flow. Or the social flow has *become* material. Buttons are money, pocketknives are money. That is, money has won. The narrator of *Hunger* of course needs money badly, but his position outside society places him outside money too, so that he sees it from a distance and at times seems to live in the kind of nostalgic, childlike world where money is always play money. This world has its demonic side, though, which is simply the world of human subjectivity cut off from meaningful intercourse with other human beings and so forced to feed on itself, on its own highly charged and paranoid energy.

Apparently nothing could be more the opposite of this world than that of Henry James. And this is true; James is the last great novelist of manners. But as we shall see, everything in *Hunger* lies dormant like a seed in James, as indeed it couldn't help but do, especially in the late Henry James, perched as he was on the brink of a strange new century.

Chapter Seven

Labor and Leisure:
The Wings of the Dove

For there to be leisure there has to be work, just as for there to be rich people there have to be poor people—and vice versa. The one thing the rich and poor have in common is money. The poor possess it as a precious dream, while the rich try not to pay too much public attention to it. "Money must be so far beneath a gentleman that it is hardly worth troubling about," says Alexis in *The Gambler*. Of course it helps for such a gentleman to be rich. It is hardly worth troubling about because it contains a reminder of poverty and squalor; that is, it contains its own lack as a nightmare always ready to surface. For the rich this reminder is often displaced from people, from those who are actually poor, and takes the form of a certain squeamish feeling about money itself, as if it could soil one's fingers. If money is sordid, then it is a suitable and appropriate sign of the life of the poor. That is, it is sordid precisely because poor people desire it. The rich, on the other hand, prefer to shy away from such a manifest object of desire, at least publicly, since they are people whose desires have supposedly been gratified. We've all heard stories about the millionaire who has no money in his pockets for a cab and lets his poorer friend pay the fare. Money does not concern him. But this disregard for money occurs with a full consciousness of the stuffed coffers that guarantee the worth and value one need not display; money is the open secret of the life of leisure.[1]

No one knew this better than Henry James, and it is to James that we shall look for the last word on money. James didn't often write about poor people, of course; *The Princess Casamassima* is the notable exception, and we may wonder after reading it whether James didn't "take up" the poor and the social question much like the Princess herself, only (presumably) to drop it later on. As we shall see, he could not drop it; its taint came off on his hands. A key to James's famous late style lies in the apparent sublimation of the sordid and greasy by style itself, by the florid, "worked-up" surface that both masks and discloses the shabby materials beneath. One often senses in James, early and late, that the sordidness of work and poverty lurks as a threat around the edges of his world. "Yes, that's the bore of comfort," Lord Warburton says in *The Portrait of a Lady*, "we only know when we're uncomfortable." Comfort, which is purchased by money, is freedom from desire. One desires it in order not to have to desire anything. James shows that this is the most obsessive desire of all, to be free of desire; it is never innocent, polite, or noble, qualities deferred to that future state of leisure in which nothing will be needed. First we must obtain money, *then* we can be innocent. But skulking around the state of leisure, like tradesmen and unscrupulous characters around a great house, are all the qualities leisure excludes: the necessity to compromise, to be low, to attack and seize, to be predatory. From Morris Townsend to Gilbert Osmond to Kate Croy, the fortune hunter is James's recurring version of the threat of poverty and its potential ugliness. The fortune hunter is James's laborer, as we shall see; repeatedly in *The Wings of the Dove*, characters talk about "working" each other. At the same time, James's fortune hunters are impoverished ladies or gentlemen of leisure

[1]This is the constant theme of Veblen's *Theory of the Leisure Class.*

who possess decorous tastes and manners without the economic means to fulfill them. If "one has to ask," as Frank O'Connor does, "what 'money' in these novels means,"[2] these novels being those of Henry James, one has to ask it because money in James is apparently schizophrenic. On the one hand, it is something released from labor and the means of production; James makes a point of not naming the source of his American characters' fortunes, as though to do so would be shameful.[3] On the other hand, money is something too many people need and are willing to do anything to obtain—willing even to "work" for, as long as the work doesn't soil their fingers.

Before we turn to *The Wings of the Dove*, these two sides of the money question in James must be explored a bit further. By the time we get to James, the nineteenth-century transition from gold to paper money is all but complete; this means that money is never palpable, never something one sees or touches—at least in James. One sees its effects, however, not only in the houses and objects with which characters in his novels surround themselves, but in their social lives, their manners, behavior, talk. In James money has become almost purely a social force, all the more so now that society, especially "good" society, has lost a great deal of its economic base (which used to be in land) and has come to depend upon new influxes of money from overseas, like blood transfusions. After the first few novels, the Europeans in James generally welcome the Americans with open arms, especially if their money has been disinfected of any smell of the work that earned it. Money in James may have a history of manufacture behind it, but by the time we arrive at it it is in the process of

---

[2]Frank O'Connor, *The Mirror in the Roadway* (New York: Knopf, 1956), p. 233.

[3]Shameful indeed; according to Fredric Jameson the origin of the Newsome fortune in *The Ambassadors* was the manufacture of chamber pots. *Marxism and Form: Twentieth Century Dialectical Theories of Literature* (Princeton: Princeton University Press, 1971), p. 167.

being absorbed into the life of leisure, often in the form of an inheritance. A few of James's characters are bankers or doctors, but, as with Dr. Sloper in *Washington Square*, the work performed by such a professional is presumed to be its own reward: "The fact of his having married a rich woman made no difference in the line he had traced for himself, and he cultivated his profession with as definite a purpose as if he still had no other resources. . . . This purpose had not been preponderantly to make money—it had been rather to learn something and to do something." Behind this description lies the very concept of a profession, service to society performed by a gentleman who just happens to be paid for his work; as Trollope notes about Dr. Thorne, "a physician should take his fee without letting his left hand know what the right hand was doing."

In other words, money in James is a sign of the life of leisure, which by definition excludes what is low or common, such as work. But money in James also comes to be haunted by this very reality it excludes, which drags behind it as a kind of shadow. This reality can be summed up in one word: sordid. Money is sordid in James whenever someone wants or needs it, *because* someone wants or needs it. The desire for money is generally not capable, as other desires in James are, of being ennobled by renunciation, because it is too interested in the fruits of desire to ever become refined or stylized. This is more true of Morris Townsend than of Kate Croy—the fortune hunter in James becomes more complex and ambiguous in the later novels—but it is a truth even Kate finally cannot escape. The desire for money is sordid to the degree that one becomes subject to it rather than making it subject to oneself. As Gilbert Osmond says in *The Portrait of a Lady*, "money is a horrid thing to follow, but a charming thing to meet." His own sordidness becomes evident only later in the novel, when we learn that he has been following it all along.

The desire for money, in other words, is soiled from the beginning by the lack that gives rise to it. Only those who *already* possess money may partake of its magnificance, indeed, its magnanimity. For them money is a form of freedom, a state of being cut off not only from material want but from labor, indebtedness, or strings of any kind—cut off from the sordid world. The problem is that those who possess it must do something with it; often this means they must give it away. Between the rich and the impoverished in James arises a mediating figure, the beneficiary. Much of James in fact is a variation of the benefactor theme in *Great Expectations*, particularly *The Portrait of a Lady* and *The Wings of the Dove*. Both Isabel Archer and Milly Theale—one a beneficiary, the other a benefactor—are compared to birds, because for the wealthy person money is the freedom of soaring and flying, of meeting the demands of one's imagination. "To be rich was a virtue," Isabel Archer decides, "because it was to be able to *do*." Of course she turns out to be wrong on both counts. To be rich is not a virtue unless one is born rich and one's money never changes hands; to *become* rich seems to be the problem, for then, like a bird, one gets caught and placed in a cage. Similarly, Milly Theale, who is precious, odd, beautiful, fragile, deep, and free like an exotic, colorful bird—who is above all literally a treasure or, as Mrs. Stringham thinks, a mine—is at the same time the prey of those who don't have money. Every time money presents the possibility of freedom in James, it turns over and shows its other face, that of bondage. Every time it seems cut off from matter and appears to be airy or lofty or bright, it becomes from another point of view slippery and sticky. The two sides of money in James, then, are actually one side subverted by the other. Leisure and labor, wealth and poverty are linked by an absolute necessity. If money never had to change hands, it wouldn't present these problems; the wealthy would be wealthy and the poor poor. But people lose money or desire it or, worse, want to give it away—as Ralph Touchett convinces his father to do, as Milly Theale decides to do (staving off death until her gift to Merton Densher can be received on Christmas Eve—one of James's more macabre touches), and even as Isabel Archer thinks she is doing in marrying Gilbert Osmond. That is, Isabel decides Osmond is a gentleman in possession of excellent taste and so feels comforted that the money that is part of the gift of herself will be in good hands. Her reasoning is similar to Ralph Touchett's and turns out to be as disastrous. In *The Portrait of a Lady*, money has a double face that comes up single: in the guise of grace, it is actually a curse.

The Wings of the Dove is similar, though with unprecedented complexity it integrates the sordidness of money into the very world of beauty and leisure that seems to exclude it. Flawed as it is, it is still James's most powerful novel on the money theme, and its language is just as haunting as it is annoying, and necessarily so; as we shall see, this language whose fumes cannot be eased out of the room is itself a kind of material production, rooted for all its fussy beauty in the greasy world of the marketplace and of labor.

In stripping down the opening sentences of *The Wings of the Dove* in the following passage, I make no claim that they ever existed in this state at any stage of composition. My intention is to isolate some of those elements that define James's late style. This, then, is not the opening page of *The Wings of the Dove*, nor could it have been; but the words are all James's own, in the order in which he wrote them:

> She waited for her father to come in, but he kept her uncon-scionably, and there were moments at which she showed her-self in the glass a face positively pale with the irritation that had brought her to the point of going away without sight of him. It was at this point that she remained, moving from the shabby sofa to the armchair upholstered in a cloth that gave at once the sense of the slippery and the sticky. She had looked at the sallow prints on the walls and at the magazine that enhanced the effect of the purplish cloth on the table; she had above all taken a brief stand on the balcony to which the pair of long

windows gave access. The vulgar little street offered scant re-
lief from the vulgar little room; its office was to suggest to her
that the narrow black house-fronts constituted quite the publicity implied by such privacies. One felt them in the room
exactly as one felt the room in the street. Each time she turned
in again and gave him up, it was to sound to a deeper depth the
failure of fortune and honour.

This is unmistakably James, but it sounds like middle James,
the James of *The Portrait of a Lady* or *The Princess Casamassima*.
It glides, it specifies, but it plays coy too. It *suggests*. It talks
about a "deeper depth" but also mentions a shabby sofa. Effects are "enhanced" in the eye of (in this version) the nameless
observer; attitudes are struck, judgments are made, qualities
are named: the street and room are "vulgar," the cloth "slippery and sticky." We do not need to have this observer's
revulsion named, for it colors all she observes. And that is as it
should be, since this is Henry James.

But it isn't what he wrote, and the restored version, if
wordy by comparison, is telling:

> She waited, Kate Croy, for her father to come in, but he kept
> her unconscionably, and there were moments at which she
> showed herself, in the glass over the mantle, a face positively
> pale with the irritation that had brought her to the point of
> going away without sight of him. It was at this point, however,
> that she remained; changing her place, moving from the shab-
> by sofa to the armchair upholstered in a glazed cloth that gave
> at once—she had tried it—the sense of the slippery and of the
> sticky. She had looked at the sallow prints on the walls and at
> the lonely magazine, a year old, that combined, with a small
> lamp in coloured glass and a knitted white centrepiece wanting
> in freshness, to enhance the effect of the purplish cloth on the
> principal table; she had above all from time to time taken a brief
> stand on the small balcony to which the pair of long windows
> gave access. The vulgar little street, in this view, offered scant
> relief from the vulgar little room; its main office was to suggest

to her that the narrow black house-fronts, adjusted to a standard that would have been low even for backs, constituted quite the publicity implied by such privacies. One felt them in the room exactly as one felt the room—the hundred like it or worse—in the street. Each time she turned in again, each time, in her impatience, she gave him up, it was to sound to a deeper depth, while she tasted the faint, flat emanation of things, the failure of fortune and of honour.

This is unmistakably *late* James, and the reasons should be obvious: it bristles with qualifying phrases, appositional clauses, adjectives, interruptions, explanations—all the paraphernalia of the parenthetical style whose thick pigment often obscures its figures, at least until the eye adjusts. That is, everything is heavily colored; the magazine is "lonely," the centerpiece "wanting in freshness," and the lamp, the sofa, the glazed cloth, the street express not only shabbiness—the failure of fortune—but shame, the failure of honor. But we don't know why; we never in fact learn what it is that Kate Croy's father has *done*. Origins in James are unnamed not because he declines to believe in them, but because their rippling effects are what count: not the name of Milly's disease, but the way she and others react to it; not what it was that Mrs. Newsome's family in *The Ambassadors* manufactured, but the power of her money. In this passage it becomes clear that a direct link exists between the year-old magazine, the centerpiece wanting in freshness, the slippery and sticky cloth, and the failure of fortune and honor; objects speak, the material world is an expressive phantasmagoria. But they speak with the aid of a florid manner that at first glance seems meant to sublimate by style the sordid things noted. In James, those origins that remain unnamed invariably are shameful or distasteful; so the sordid too can be recognized only by its effects, by the rippling way it spreads to touch things apparently not directly related to it. Thus—and it may take several readings—we come to recognize with a gradual shock that this florid manner doesn't sublimate the sordid; indeed, like everything else, it *expresses* it. Its "beauty," if we may grant it that, is inseparable from a kind of corruption, from the ugliness of the failure of fortune and honor.

This is all very conscious and deliberate, as James's explicit references to Kate's beauty in the opening passages make clear. Waiting for her father, she glances in the mirror. Her beauty, James tells us, is apparently not linked to her father's corruption. "Was it not in fact the partial escape from this 'worst' in which she was steeped to be able to make herself out again as agreeable to see? . . . If she saw more things than her fine face in the dull glass of her father's lodgings, she might have seen that, after all, she was not herself a fact in the collapse. She didn't judge herself cheap, she didn't make for misery. Personally, at least, she was not chalk-marked for the auction." She isn't chalk-marked for the auction because (as we subsequently learn), although she has been "taken up" by her aunt, she will not allow herself to be married to *any* mere aristocrat who comes along; she is not chalk-marked for Lord Mark. She secretly engages herself to Merton Densher not because she judges herself cheap, but because she loves him, because he is handsome and smart and good, even though penniless like herself. Thus the problem of the novel unfolds: how will this beauty, whom at least five people are depending on for money to redeem their relative poverty—how will she obtain the money to make her marriage, satisfy her family, and retain her self-respect? Of course, she cannot. It is impossible, and James's florid style, knocking continually against its own material limits, dramatizes the impossibility. The beautiful face Kate notes in her father's dull mirror is so hemmed in by the greasy and sticky and sallow that it cannot help but finally be touched by them. Kate's beauty, James's language, Kate's very surname: these are all precious things that have sustained a wound, and the wound is material reality. Pacing the room, she thinks about her name, her father's name, dragged down by the failure of fortune and honor. *Croy*, all the things around her say. "It was the name, above all, she would take in hand—

the precious name she so liked and that, in spite of the harm her wretched father had done it, was not yet past praying for. She loved it in fact the more tenderly for that bleeding wound. But what could a penniless girl do with it but let it go?" To escape the sordid world, penniless Kate must change her name. Yet, as we've seen, she conceives of herself as not chalk-marked for the auction. The attempt to have her cake and eat it—the cake in this case is her honor—naturally fails, and James's version of that common theme in the nineteenth-century novel, the necessity to marry for money, turns upon this paradox: that escaping the sordidness of poverty by pursuing money lands one squarely within the sordidness of money. The clear link between the sordid, money, and a certain condition of language—language that may be worked up, layered with qualifications, dressed up for display, but that still cannot escape the greasy and sticky—is thus made from the novel's beginning. And James's late manner, which *appears* like Kate's father to be the "least connected with anything unpleasant," is consequently shown to be rooted in the most unpleasant things.

James's late manner is a linguistic process that repeatedly interrupts itself at crucial points—between the noun and the verb, between the auxiliary and the main verb, between the verb and its object—with modifiers and parenthetical clauses. At its worst in *The Wings of the Dove*, it can sound like this: "She might, he was not unaware, have made out, from some deep part of her, the bearing, in respect to herself, of the little fact he had announced." This stammering accuracy makes of the sentence something fussy and halting, a process willfully laborious. Why? To begin with, such language exists to *qualify*—because nothing is simple, everything mixed. For example, Kate needs money but doesn't want to marry for it. She is unlike her father, but like him too. Kate and her father thus defer and displace each other, as do Kate and Milly, Kate and Densher, Aunt Maud and Lord Mark, and so forth. The characters exist to qualify each other, to define each other by substitution, and these forces erupt in the novel's language too. The parenthetical style is a process of perpetual deferment and displacement masking a multiplicity, like water always just on the point of boiling. We often sense the urge toward definition in James's long paragraphs; this is in fact their usual principle of organization. But in the apparent service of precision and accuracy, all the displacing phrases, substitutions, and qualifications have the effect of spreading everything out, of making attribution, for example, nearly impossible to fix. The characters of *The Wings of the Dove* indeed have much at stake in the novel's style, since its shorelessness seems to absolve them from responsibility or, in a sense, to collectivize their responsibility, which they share with sofas, mist, gondolas, Italian servants, and each other. If the style is suggestive, it is often because, whipped out of itself like froth, there appears to be nothing to suggest, and everything could apparently dissolve in the air—unless we have a coarse word from Lord Mark or a bald question from Merton Densher. For example, "Since she's to die I'm to marry her?" Densher asks Kate. "So that when her death has taken place I shall in the natural course have money?" The style exists to qualify, because schemes like this are shared responsibilities, things that cannot be named until it is too late, until the name has spread its roots everywhere, into everyone.

We might say, furthermore, that James's late style exists to halt process, to create a kind of stillness of design. Design is evidently important in James, and we can sense it in sentences like this one from the opening paragraph: "She tried to be sad so as not to be angry, but it made her angry that she couldn't be sad." Such rhetoric is nearly Elizabethan (and therefore Roman), but it cannot halt the grinding forth of the language. If sentences like this momentarily check the sense of process in order to create a still design, the design nonetheless becomes eroded from within by the very laborious nature of that process. Parallelisms, we sense, are resting places for James, brief pauses in the sentences' effort to proceed through all their qualifications and layers of negation. The urge toward parallel construction is certainly there, but it generally is not an organizing principle as it is, say, in Dickens. Not repetition, but lateral movement, dissemination, the continuous production of a rippling current seems essential. Still, this current encounters obstacles and blockages. It must labor to achieve the billowing movement that seems natural to it. At times it seems to be doodling, to be tracing its designs at leisure, playfully; but the gentleman novelist, who wrote in his leisure time, wrote a book that "might have a great deal to give, but would probably ask for equal services in return" (the preface). In other words, he transformed play into the highest form of work.

We sense in the opening passages of *The Wings of the Dove* that the sordid reality being named is also being sifted through interpretive layers. Yet the effect is not to obscure or veil it. Among all its qualifications, "the faint, flat emanation of things" exists as the limit of everything language can do to the world, everything language can stylize, the limit of its utmost ingenuity. It lies present *in* the language like a canvas unraveling, simultaneously unweaving what the painting weaves and thus refusing to be taken up into the design, to be "worked." What art cannot redeem is the product of mere labor, whose material nature leaks, as it were, as though the produced thing would never be dry, would always remain "slippery" and "sticky" ("greasy" is used on the following page). Of course art *can* work things up, can create ingenious surfaces. In chapter 2 we learn that Kate now "saw as she had never seen before how material things spoke to her. She saw, and she blushed to see, that if in contrast with some of its old aspects life now affected her as a dress successfully 'done up,' this was exactly by reason of the trimmings and lace, was a matter of ribbons and silk and velvet." This is said of Aunt Maud's house, a place where the greasy and sticky are absent. Yet the special vulgarity of Aunt Maud's objects also becomes evident in this and other passages, and no ingenious labor can disguise it;

indeed, it is a *form* of ingenuity. In Merton Densher's eyes, the things in Aunt Maud's house, Lancaster Gate, "constituted an order and abounded in rare material—precious woods, metals, stuffs, stones. He had never dreamed of anything so fringed and scalloped, so buttoned and corded, drawn everywhere so tight and curled everywhere so thick. He had never dreamed of so much gilt and glass, so much satin and plush, so much rosewood and marble and malachite. But it was above all the solid forms, the wasted finish, the misguided cost, the general attestation of morality and money, a good conscience and big balance." This image of material reality erupting from the midst of all its worked-up forms is central to the novel and crucial for understanding James's late manner. We sense material things being de-signed, de-processed, in order to uncover their fundamental purpose: to display the wealth of their owner. This is parallel to the strategy of the novel's opening passage, in which the poverty (and shame) of the owner of those objects is displayed. In both cases matter *speaks*, wells up from within the ingenious surface, "so fringed and scalloped, so buttoned and corded, drawn everywhere so tight and curled everywhere so thick," of its manifest language.

Matter speaks, yet language breaks down in this novel. Beneath the finely textured surface of the language lie gaps, things that cannot be named: Milly's disease, the shame of Kate's father, Kate's scheme to obtain Milly's money. James's use of such disjunctions or gaps is not only for suggestiveness or, as he puts it in his preface, for the indirect presentation of the image. The gaps are also there to invite us to continually read back through the language to its limits, just as in the passage quoted above we are invited to observe, through Densher's eyes, a kind of deconstruction of Aunt Maud's objects, their reversion to more atavistic states, "so much rosewood and marble and malachite." Those objects are never named and are barely described before they are stripped of their status as objects, submitted to the hammer—reduced to raw material. Matter speaks bluntly, stubbornly, its one or two words. This happens also in the section in Venice, where, after having been turned away from Milly's house, Densher wanders the streets and notices the "rubbish in shops," the "greasy" pavement, "the tables and chairs that overflowed from the cafés," and in general "the broken charm of the world . . . broken into smaller pieces." Behind the language of this novel as well as behind its representation of settings and places lies an absolute sense of material limits. The seemingly self-generating, "worked-up" surface of the language could break down at any moment, we sense, like a machine with a wrench thrown into it. Still, it doesn't break down; like the characters themselves, it remains under control. But the effect is to suggest the very fragile nature of that control, to make it clear that, just as the characters beneath their glazed surface could literally become predators—tigers or panthers—so the language could break down into smaller and smaller pieces, the excessive number of commas could close in, and the words revert to babble.

In other words, the subtext of leisure is the sordid and the predatory, just as the subtext of James's high style is the opacity of nonsense. When we see art in James we also perceive labor, just as when we see wealth we also see poverty. James's brief homage to Gissing from which I have already quoted is written with an uncomfortably superior, tongue-in-cheek irony precisely because, of all his contemporaries, Gissing was the one who most resembled him, though the resemblance at times took the form of a negative image. And the attraction was mutual; Gissing admired James. His neglected little gem of a novel, *Eve's Ransom*, could have been written by James, though its typically Jamesian situations have been transposed to the lower classes. As in *The Portrait of a Lady*, a poor woman in *Eve's Ransom* is ransomed by money, taught finer things, learns repose, satisfaction, and enjoyment, only to have the gift spoil her life. And as in *The Portrait*, self-denial and self-control become the rewards of a life spoiled by money and in this case by its subsequent lack, though in *Eve's Ransom* the rewards accrue not to the beneficiary but to the benefactor, Hilliard. Like James, Gissing created powerful women characters, and like James he was obsessed not only by the money theme in general, but by the conflicting social claims and costs of labor and leisure. His *Nether World* could be thought of as a negative of *The Wings of the Dove*, though more clumsy and obvious in its effects. The London poor in *The Nether World* ape their betters; their most conspicuous standard of judgment is respectability. White collars, for example, "put in vogue by aristocratic sanction," become an important mark of the microcosmic class divisions *within* the working class. The poor in *The Nether World*, Gissing tells us, "can seldom command privacy; their scenes alike of tenderness and of anger must for the most part be enacted on the peopled ways." This is touching enough, but more so perhaps if we recall that it is exactly the situation of Densher and Kate in *The Wings of the Dove*, forced to snatch intimate moments in public squares while their friends are busy in shops. Like Hilliard in *Eve's Ransom*, Densher must rent a room in which he and his lover can meet, though the cost of it, as we shall see, turns out to be more than he bargained for.

In *The Nether World*, Gissing continually reminds us "that the differences between the nether and the upper world are purely superficial," because the dominant motive in both is money hunger. Thus the netherworld is populated by predators; Clem pursues Joe Snowdon for the money she thinks he possesses, and Joe stalks his own father for his money. Joe's "vicious lower lip" marks him as a kind of savage, and Clem's mother, Mrs. Peckover, becomes as "excited by the scent of money as a jackal by that of carrion." Similar metaphors appear in *The Wings of the Dove*. One effect of the title's metaphor is to make it clear that, if Milly is a dove, she therefore constitutes an opportunity for predators. Repeatedly, Aunt Maud is compared to a lioness; alone with Kate, Milly feels herself "with a creature who paced like a panther." When the others talk of the absent Milly at dinner, Mrs. Stringham imagines she is watching her friend being martyred in an arena, not by lions and tigers but by "domestic animals let loose for the joke." Within domestic politeness lies rapacity, just as within leisure lies work. In *The Nether World* the laboring classes are an ironic aristocracy, a grotesque parody of the upper classes, while in *The Wings of the Dove* the middle and upper classes are workers in disguise. "Nobody here, you know, does anything for nothing," says Lord Mark. "You must work it, you know," Kate's father tells her. "He was working Lancaster Gate for all it was worth: just as it was, no doubt, working *him*, and just as the working and the worked were in London, as one might explain, the parties to every relation." The "he" in this case is Merton Densher, whose situation is being explained to him by Kate. "The worker in one connexion was the worked in another; it was as broad as it was long—with the wheels of the system, as might be seen, wonderfully oiled." In this service economy, of course, people must pay. Milly, indeed, will "pay a hundred per cent," says Kate—"and even to the end, doubtless, through the nose." Milly will pay because she finds herself surrounded by the likes of Aunt Maud and Lord Mark, the former "Britannia of the Market Place," and the latter someone who "weighed it out in ounces." Indeed, "each of the pair [Aunt Maud and Lord Mark] was really waiting for what the other would put down." And all of them, including Kate and Densher, find their telling reflection in Eugenio, who "was for ever carrying one well-kept Italian hand to his heart and plunging the other straight into [Milly's] pocket."

The commerical metaphors in the novel, and the overriding metaphor of the marketplace, have previously been noted by critics.[4] In the kind of service economy James describes, one action is inevitably answered by a parallel one or by an ex-

<hr>

[4]Chiefly by Alfred Habegger in "Reciprocity and the Market Place in *The Wings of the Dove* and *What Maisie Knew*," *Nineteenth-Century Fiction* 25 (1971):455–473. See also Jan W. Dietrichson, *The Image of Money in the American Novel of the Gilded Age* (Oslo and New York: Humanities Press, 1969), especially pp. 84–86, 113–124, and 159–160, and Bradford Booth, "Henry James and the Economic Motif," *Nineteenth-Century Fiction* 8 (1953):141–150.

change, by payment. Behind the mutual compulsion and coercion of the characters' actions—the way their predatory behavior comes to be *shared*—lies the self-balancing mechanisms of the marketplace, a nearly impersonal movement of actions and reactions that operate according to the "laws" of supply and demand. Britannia herself (Aunt Maud) presides and serves the function of matching the penniless and the wealthy so that the benefits of leisure may not abandon those born into its class. But though she presides, there is still something anonymous and self-generating about it all, as there is in James's style. A "current" is said to take up Densher and urge him in a certain direction, and one of the chief moral questions of the novel is who bears responsibility for this current. Is it truly an impersonal social force—like capitalism—or is it something that some people more than others set in motion—like capitalism?

To answer this question, we must focus upon Merton Densher and his relationship to the society by which he finds himself taken up. In *The Wings of the Dove* we are given no reason to doubt the initial innocence of Densher's ignorance, because it is also ours. *We* drift on the current of this society too, a society, with its skillful counterpoint of naming and withholding, that finds its highest embodiment in James's late manner. With language itself as its chief expression, the social world in the later James is a dense human labyrinth of intention and deception, spread out across a surface as fine and laterally "deep"—that is, intricate—as a spider web. Densher finds himself caught on this surface, struggling to move but unaware even of his own motives or goals. In James, intentions are so diaphanous and layered, their solidity so attenuated, that it becomes nearly impossible to say where they begin or end, or even whose intentions they are. Densher's intentions in fact turn out to be Kate's and Mrs. Lowder's. His rejection of Milly's money at the end of the novel is a rejection of society because that is the only way he can discover where his self begins and ends. He has been too spread out and diffused, and he feels the need not simply to discover but to declare his own limits. It is in this sense, actually, that James is very much a realist, according to the definition I offered in chapter 4. He creates characters whose world overflows their experience of it and becomes something alien, an object outside them. But realism is usually a decision in James, because the conditions of his characters' egoism or ignorance are such that their selfhood often has no boundary or limit and moves outward to fill up all the corners of their world—to become in fact synonymous with it. This is Densher's problem, and it is not unlike the initial description of Madame Merle in *The Portrait of a Lady:* "She had become too flexible, too useful, was too ripe and too final. She was in a word too perfectly the social animal." This problem of the social animal is a recurring one in James. Densher's flexibility and usefulness turn out to be as immoral as the unwavering determination of those who make use of him. He has become their tool in the effort to "work" Milly. The irony of James's vocabulary becomes clear only when Densher renounces the life of leisure for that—we have to assume—of work. Only then will the world become an object again rather than an extension of his boundless self.

In James the moral act usually entails a rejection of community, and this may very well be a belated recognition of the isolation of the individual in the world of advanced capitalism. One senses a double bind in James: you can give yourself to the social world and thereby lose yourself, or you can renounce society and thereby lose all communal ties. In a sense this is the central question of realism: Where does the self end and the world begin? The issues are presented very clearly in the brief debate between Madame Merle and Isabel in *The Portrait of a Lady.* "What shall we call our 'self'?" asks the former. "Where does it begin? Where does it end? It overflows into everything that belongs to us—and then it flows back again. I know a large part of myself is in the clothes I choose to wear." This sounds reasonable, perhaps, but so does Isabel's reply: "I don't agree with you. I think just the other way. I don't know whether I succeed in expressing myself, but I know that nothing else expresses me. Nothing that belongs to me is any measure of me; everything's on the contrary a limit, a barrier, and a perfectly arbitrary one." Isabel's declaration of the self's isolation sounds noble, and by the novel's end it takes the familiar form (in James) of renunciation. What we don't see in James—except in the form of a subtext, an inner limit—is the result of such renunciation. Repeatedly, characters are brought to the choice of renunciation and the fact of isolation at the *conclusions* of his novels, when we shall no longer be with them. If the "faint, flat emanation of things" nearly overwhelms Kate at the beginning of *The Wings of the Dove*, nearly makes her run, it is because this material world, this *ordinary* world, is the one she and all the rest of the characters will be set down in at the novel's end. It is there from the beginning, running beneath the text, in Milly's disease, in the greasy and sticky objects of Mr. Croy's flat, in the odor of boiled food at the Condrips' house, in the "great glaze" of Aunt Maud's "surface"—indeed, in her "prodigious personality"—but in fact it exists (again, in Isabel Archer's words) as "a limit, a barrier, and a perfectly arbitrary one." Once the self has been sifted through the social world, it is left with this material one.

Renunciation in James is thus strangely a form of self-assertion. One renounces the social world in order to live beyond the demands of language and of others, to live *within* oneself, with only one's honor for comfort. Isabel Archer, Milly Theale, Fleda Vetch, Merton Densher: for all of them, self-assertion and self-sacrifice are inseparable. The best example is Milly, a variation of Isabel Archer's character by way of Daisy Miller's fate. In *The Wings of the Dove*, Milly serves others in the guise of allowing them to help her, and she does this conscious that they think they are using her in the guise of serving her. Rich and dying, she appears to be passive, a sacrificial lamb, but her self-will becomes ferocious even, or especially, after she has "turned her face to the wall"—that is, after she has renounced the social world for the material one, for her own death. Until the novel's end, Merton Densher appears to be passive too, though his passivity is largely the effect of ignorance. He seems to be the least greedy of the novel's characters, with the exception of Milly, yet his lack of money finally injects a commercial spirit into his relationship with Kate that effectively separates them in the guise of uniting them. Milly, by contrast—and here we sense James's homage to wealth—says everyone thinks too much about money, to which Mrs. Stringham replies that indifference to it comes easier to some than to others. Milly can allow herself to be used precisely because she is wealthy; she can spend and give away money without giving herself away. Densher, on the other hand, is forced to buy Kate and sell himself. Only after she comes to his rooms and surrenders to him sexually will he agree to carry out her wishes with respect to Milly, "as a service for which the price named by him had been magnificently paid." They sell themselves to each other, as serious a sin as their pursuit of Milly, and Densher's belated penance is to renounce Milly's money. He gives Kate the choice between the money and him, and the novel ends just as his world is about to become ordinary.

Renunciation in James may be noble and may even be "moral," as so many of his commentators assert, but it is hardly pleasant, and its effects (for James at least) are incapable of becoming the subject of fiction. In James the world (as opposed to society) begins at the conclusion of a book. We sense the cameras panning back, the traffic of material things honking and beeping, the twentieth century beginning—all just beyond the novel's grasp. This ordinary world is also the merely economic world, one in which labor accumulates wealth in piecemeal ways and money is no longer the opportunity to display magnificence, spur desire, play God, soar, or fall. In a certain respect its representative in *The Wings of the Dove* is Eugenio, a servant, the only character in the novel who institutionalizes the service economy within which all the characters operate. For a price (his hand is always in Milly's pocket), his function is to protect Milly and her friends from distasteful economic negotiations. As a servant in the service of wealth, he stands for what Densher has allowed himself to become. Thus Densher recognizes his guilt in Eugenio's eyes, sees himself for the first time as a fortune hunter when Eugenio observes him: "One had come to a queer pass when a servant's opinion so mattered. Eugenio's would have mattered even if, as founded on a low vision of appearances, it had been quite wrong. It was more disagreeable accordingly that the vision of appearances was quite right, and was scarcely less low." In a novel in which everyone "works" someone else, Eugenio and Densher are the only paid employees, the only ones on salary. It may be too strong to say that Densher will become an English Eugenio after the novel's final page, but the similarities between the characters are impossible to ignore.

What Kate will become is another question. One is tempted to say an Aunt Maud, but Aunt Maud is clearly a Philistine, and Kate is not. In the novel's opening chapter, James several times makes the point that, looking in her father's mirror, Kate sees something other than herself. "She stared into the tarnished glass too hard indeed to be staring at her beauty alone." Later in the same paragraph, she decides she will take up her father's name, "the precious name she so liked and that, in spite of the harm her wretched father had done it, was not yet past praying for." When her father finally appears, he turns out to be one of the slimiest characters in all of James. But the telling passage is this one, just after he walks in: "The one stray gleam of comedy just now in his daughter's eyes was the absurd feeling he momentarily made her have of being herself 'looked up' by him in sordid lodgings. For a minute after he came in it was as if the place were her own and he the visitor with susceptibilities." In a novel in which the characters act as surrogates and substitutes for each other—surrogate lovers, surrogate laborers—the revenge reality takes upon such games is to fix the players in place, cut off in their costumes. From one point of view they are displaced and dispossessed, but from another they come into their own inheritance, they take up their proper names. The face Kate sees in the mirror is of course her father's; and the novel is the story of how she becomes a Croy.

Financiers, Counterfeiters, and the Modern Novel

In the twentieth century, money has won. But oddly enough, fewer novels dealing with money have been written in this century, though this epilogue will touch upon some of the obvious exceptions—the novels of Dreiser, Fitzgerald's *The Great Gatsby*, Wharton's *The House of Mirth*, and Gide's *Les faux-monnayeurs*. Of course the money theme has not stopped cropping up, and it will not; in recent years we've had Bellow's and Doctorow's novels, Gaddis's *J. R.*, Updike's *Rabbit is Rich*. But much of the tension is gone from it.[1] Increasingly, money signals the presence of parody or satire in fiction, not the presence of a complex social vision. The complex social vision is lacking precisely because money has won, because

---

[1] For an opposing view, especially with regard to modern American fiction, see *Money Talks: Language and Lucre in American Fiction*, ed. Roy R. Male (Norman: University of Oklahoma Press, 1980). Most of the essays in this collection, however, implicitly or explicitly recognize the heterogeneous nature of modern fiction, in contrast to fiction of the nineteenth century. For example, David S. Gross in his essay on Doctorow: "Modern literary response is more diverse than that in nineteenth-century realist fiction. In some modern novels the [money] question is avoided entirely, as writers have sought to separate their works as much as possible from material reality." *Money Talks*, p. 78.

our economic life is more all-embracing, our class divisions more economic. If the nineteenth-century novel traces the erosion of customary values by the democratizing force of money, the twentieth-century novel—when it cares to—traces the futile attempt to read customary values back into money, to imagine that money signals human worth. Such transparent nostalgia can only become the subject of satire. New York society in *The House of Mirth* or *The Great Gatsby* is thinner, more superficial, more easily dismissed than the society it apes—nineteenth-century London's—because its pretensions are so obviously reductive. We can see in such a "society" the way money, like a vast reservoir, has drained into all its transactions, the way being has so thoroughly become having. As a result, the society novel simply disappears after the first two or three decades of the twentieth century; its last great monument is probably Proust. Class divisions have turned promiscuous in proportion as money has made its presence so ubiquitous as to become nearly invisible. Certainly, one of the reasons we don't notice money as much in twentieth-century fiction is that it is everywhere. When class divisions are determined almost exclusively by money, their quantitative nature becomes clear to everyone, and hypocrisy is virtually impossible. Thus the novel of manners gradually gives way to the novel of single consciousness, a change whose results we have already seen in Hamsun's *Hunger*. That is, in the twentieth century the only alternative to a purely material world becomes not manners, but subjectivity.

In an embryonic way we can also see this in Edith Wharton's *The House of Mirth*, that curiously powerful novel with one foot in the nineteenth century and one in the twentieth. Beneath its Jamesian skin lies no one other than Theodore Dreiser; indeed, the scene at the end of *The House of Mirth* in which Lily Bart goes to work at Mme. Regina's little hat factory bears a resemblance to the well-known chapter in *Sister Carrie* in which Carrie works at a shoe factory. One may even read in Lily Bart's fate a paradigm of the fate of the novel of

Epilogue

manners: "Since she had been brought up to be ornamental, she could hardly blame herself for failing to serve any practical purposes." Of course the novel of manners becomes ornamental only when it loses its moral scaffolding, when money is not merely a new force to contend with, but the only force. And this is precisely the point of *The House of Mirth*. Its conflicts are not between status and wealth but between poverty (or relative poverty) and wealth, and the debts of its characters are at bottom exclusively financial. When we are told that "Bertha Dorset's social credit was based on an impregnable bank-account," we can assume this is true for all social credit in Wharton's New York. To be sure, there is a shade of a conflict between new money and old money. In the American novel— in Howells, Fitzgerald, Wharton, Dreiser, and others—the longevity of one's money often becomes an additional defining characteristic of class. When Gatsby says that Daisy's voice is full of money, the important word he leaves out (though both he and Nick assume it) is *old:* her voice is full of old money, established money, inherited money, money of the leisure class such as it exists in America. The class divisions in *The Great Gatsby* are between those who pursue money and those who don't have to pursue it. But in *The House of Mirth* the pursuers, the nouveaux riches, are accepted into society after a brief, obligatory struggle; the Wellington Brys pass the test of Newport, and even Sim Rosedale makes significant inroads into New York society.

In *The House of Mirth*, Sim Rosedale purchases a mansion on Fifth Avenue as part of his plan to enter society. If we could assume the homogeneity of fictional worlds, we might wonder if one of his neighbors wasn't Frank Cowperwood, from Dreiser's trilogy *The Financier*, *The Titan*, and *The Stoic*. Cowperwood is one of the exceptions; for all his money, he doesn't make it in society, not so much because he is a former felon as because he has a vulgar wife. Even this isn't a sufficient reason, however. We sense in Dreiser's novel an insistence that Cowperwood be lonely, isolated, a monadic personality who prefers the remote rooms of his own consciousness and his own financial fantasies to the external world. Cowperwood winds up as a stoic because, for all his material wealth, he has been, from the beginning, curiously indifferent to material things. He likes paintings and good houses, but these are means to an end: the conspicuous display of wealth. Similarly, his gas lines and streetcar franchises are material residues, as it were, of that symbolic manipulation of signifiers called high finance, which is the real subject of the first two novels in the trilogy. As John Berryman puts it in his brilliant little afterword to the Signet Classic edition of *The Titan*, "Cowperwood can make no show of decency alongside Howells' and Lewis' heroes because he is not dealing with the real world as they are. Our position here is paradoxical but helpful. Paint and real estate are real things, real business. Finance is not; it is abstract."[2]

He is not dealing with the real world. What a curious thing to say about a novel written by the master of American realism! But it is true. American novels that take money as their central concern inevitably wind up chronicling the isolation of one character, his or her separation from the real world. Lily Bart is Frank Cowperwood in reverse; without money, she grows smaller and smaller, becomes increasingly severed from the world around her, and finally disappears into herself. Hurstwood in *Sister Carrie* finds himself similarly stripped of all social and material props. In his decline, his eyes begin to hurt and he gives up reading. "He found it more and more difficult to get anything from anybody." Like a specter half in and half out of the physical world, he shuffles along the streets of New York observing the material flow of life that goes on without him, outside him; he becomes in fact a parody of those nineteenth-century observers of the social panorama in Balzac and Tolstoy—Rastignac or Levin or Pierre—the solitary figure

[2]Afterword, *The Titan* (New York: New American Library, 1965), p. 503.

for whom the sensory world has become entirely alien. From this it is only a brief step to a characteristic feature of late realism: the method of juxtaposition, which eventually becomes collage. In the final pages of *Sister Carrie*, Hurstwood, "a chronic type of bum and beggar," wanders down Broadway. Carrie, reading (what else?) *Le Père Goriot* in her room at the Waldorf, looks out the window and sees a man fall down in the snow, but fails to recognize him as Hurstwood. The contrast, of course, is similar to that in Balzac's novel, where Père Goriot is dying in squalor while his daughters frolic at a ball. It is also similar to the picture of Lily Bart walking down Fifth Avenue in utter dejection and poverty, excluded from the houses that once served her as surrogate homes. The method of collage calls for the juxtaposition of elements that fail to acknowledge or touch each other, that are caught passing in the night. At the end of *Sister Carrie*, Hurstwood, Carrie, Drouet, and Hurstwood's wife and daughter all move about within a relatively small perimeter, unaware of each other's proximity. Geographical space has become economic space, and the chief characteristic of economic space is the isolation of elements upon a two-dimensional surface. The method of collage also depends upon a third factor, an observer outside it all who perceives the irony of the juxtaposed elements. Thus late realism gives birth to the movie screen, whose first method (in Griffith and Eisenstein) is that of collage and juxtaposition (or cross-cutting) and whose art consists of creating a temporal flow that avoids transitions.

He is not dealing with the real world. Few of Dreiser's characters are, and all the more so when they are dealing with money. If money is a sign of reality in the nineteenth-century novel, it is a sign of something different in the twentieth-century novel, a sign perhaps of fantasy, or at the very least of the fantasy of power. This is an old American theme, of course, and goes back at least as far as Ahab in *Moby Dick* (one of the first American novels to take an actual industry as its setting). In Dreiser's trilogy, the character of money is explicitly identified with this ambition for power: "Few people have the sense of financial individuality strongly developed. They do not know what it means to be a controller of wealth, to have that which releases the sources of social action—its medium of exchange. They want money, but not for money's sake. They want it for what it will buy in the way of simple comforts, whereas the financier wants it for what it will control—for what it will represent in the way of dignity, force, power" (*The Financier*). Values that might counter the acquisition of power—morality, custom, religion—are shown by Dreiser to be mere talk, nothing. They are not real. Yet, strangely enough, neither is finance. "His business as he saw it was with the material facts of life, or, rather, with those third- and fourth- degree theorems and syllogisms which control material things and so represent wealth" (*The Titan*). That is, his business is with representations, and in *The Titan* the assumption increasingly is that the representations are far more important than what they represent. In his own way, Cowperwood is thus a figure of the artist. He doesn't *make* money, he *creates* it. The distinction is crucial. Polk Lynde, a minor character, is designated as "a loafer and idler who had never created in any way the money he was so freely spending." Cowperwood, on the other hand, manipulates large amounts of money in order to generate more. "Out of the cash drawers of his various companies he took immense sums, temporary loans, as it were, which later he had charged by his humble servitors to 'construction,' 'equipment,' or 'operation.' He was like a canny wolf prowling in a forest of trees of his own creation." "Construction," "equipment," "operation" are clearly ciphers, empty signifiers, and the forest of Cowperwood's own creation is consequently a fantasy, a poem, a fiction.

We've already seen this theme in the nineteenth-century novel: money is a fiction. The difference in Dreiser lies in the lack of a dialectical view, at least in *The Titan*. Reality is not so much the antithesis of the fiction of money as it is its residue.

When Cowperwood expands his financial empire, he creates the appearance of money, to which actual money eventually becomes attracted. In the stock market, he finances his purchases (while driving the market up) with their own prospective sales. Capital expands like a chain letter, by means of a manipulation of secondary representations that amounts almost to controlled combustion, and the financier must be prepared to run should it break out of control. The metaphor of the Chicago fire in *The Financier* makes this clear. In *The Titan*, Cowperwood skims his expanding capital in order to secure it; he piles up a reserve of eight or nine million dollars in houses, land, paintings, and government bonds so that when the conflagration comes he won't be burned as he was in the first volume. Only this skimmed money is actual, secure, stable, real; the rest of his money is busy creating more money. In this way the secure becomes a residue of the unstable, the real a residue of the fantastic.

Behind all this lies an assumption about money and art that is characteristic of our century. Money is not real, art is not real. Both, in Melville's (and Gide's) metaphor, are counterfeit. Or both in a sense are *presumptions* of reality, contained within the larger category of the counterfeit. Paper money of course creates this consciousness, though in the nineteenth century the sheer novelty of the power of such a representation resulted in a certain reverence for what money could do, for what it could buy. And of course we have never lost this reverence; we cling to it even while we distrust it, even while, writing our first check, we marvel at the unreality of it all.

In this respect two points need to be made. First, the realistic novel has never died but in this century has increasingly come to be included within the category of the fantastic. This is obvious in the so-called magic realists such as García Márquez, but perhaps less so in novelists like Updike or Bellow; nevertheless, the very assumptions by which the fictional worlds of Updike or Bellow or Cheever are nailed together own as much to Kafka as they do to Trollope or Tolstoy. Realism today operates under the spell of the fantastic, within its perimeters, because in fact reality does too. The century's greatest realist, Kafka, demonstrated this in the 1920s, and subsequent history has proved him correct. Second, the twentieth-century novel displays a split of the high and low made possible in part by money. Realists such as Dreiser or Lewis or the proletarian novelists of the thirties dealt with economic realities, whereas modernists such as Joyce, Gide, Proust, or Kafka—practitioners of high art all—dealt with human subjectivity, and its language, in isolation. Still, these are two sides of a single coin; the apparent lack of economic considerations in Kafka or Joyce exists by virtue of what the text excludes, and what the text excludes throws a shadow across it that becomes part of it, something Kafka for one is always highly conscious of. This may be why, with the obvious exceptions,[3] the split of high and low so pronounced at the beginning of the century is less evident today. Our best novelists are realists *and* fictionists (or surrealists, or fabulators, or postmodernists).

Whether they are also counterfeiters remains to be seen. As Gide points out, counterfeit money functions as actual until it is discovered. In our century the counterfeit artists are usually those whose assumptions one disapproves. During the transition from realism to modernism, each side would naturally regard the other as counterfeit, and we are only just beginning to emerge from such an either/or mentality. Still we fear the counterfeit, and rightly so, not because it scandalously disrespects reality—indeed, counterfeiters so *respect* reality as to pay it the highest homage, imitation—but because it creates uncertainty, ambiguity.[4] The culminating symbol of Melville's *The Confidence Man* is a counterfeit detector, whose confi-

---

[3] The obvious exceptions can be grouped under the term "experimental" writing, which apparently is a permanent legacy of modernism. By its very nature, a small percentage of experimental writing will always be interesting, even ground breaking, while the bulk of it will remain derivative—or counterfeit.

[4] Cf. Hugh Kenner: "We are deep, these days, in the counterfeit, and have long since had to forego easy criteria for what is 'real.' (And a counterfeit

dent guide to the signs distinguishing genuine and false bank notes, instead of reassuring its owner, produces the opposite effect:

> Laying the Detector square before him on the table, he then, with something of the air of an officer bringing by the collar a brace of culprits to the bar, placed two bills opposite the Detector, upon which, the examination began, lasting some time, prosecuted with no small research and vigilance. . . .
>
> "I don't know, I don't know," returned the old man, perplexed, "there's so many marks of all sorts to go by, it makes it a kind of uncertain. Here, now, is this bill," touching one, "it looks to be a three dollar bill on the Vicksburgh Trust and Insurance Banking Company. Well, the Detector says—"
>
> "But why, in this case, care what it says? Trust and Insurance! What more would you have?"
>
> "No; but the Detector says, among fifty, that, if a good bill, it must have, thickened here and there into the substance of the paper, little wavy spots of red; and it says they must have a kind of silky feel, being made by the lint of a red silk handkerchief stirred up in the paper-maker's vat—the paper being made to order for the company."
>
> "Well, and is—"
>
> "Stay. But then it adds, that sign is not always to be relied on; for some good bills get so worn, the red marks get rubbed out. And that's the case with my bill here—see how old it is— or else it's a counterfeit, or else—I don't see right—or else— dear, dear me—I don't know what else to think."

The inability to distinguish the counterfeit from the genuine naturally leads the old man to discredit his own perception— "or else—I don't see right"—but the real problem seems to be the detector itself. Without it all the old man's bills would be genuine, because he would never have occasion to question them. With it they are all brought into question, all sullied.

---

banknote is real)." *The Counterfeiters* (Bloomington: Indiana University Press, 1968), p. 20.

What kind of society needs a counterfeit detector? One in which assumptions about the real are in upheaval, one in which "that sign is not always to be relied on"—in other words, modern society, which Melville's novel prefigured by about fifty years. And as *The Confidence Man* makes clear, the detector solves nothing; it adds to the confusion instead of clarifying it. Indeed, in this case it creates the confusion, all the more so for being—as Melville strongly suggests—counterfeit itself.

Modernism discredited not only what we thought was genuine, but the standards by which we made such judgments, the detectors by which we distinguished the authentic from the counterfeit. But the question arises: Isn't the distinction a false one? Doesn't all genuine art—even to a small degree— partake of the countefeit? And the answer is yes, of course, at least in the sense that nothing is pure. Realistic narrative, as we have seen (chapter 4), conflates the artificial, or theatrical, and the real. Its conventions constitute a code, a rhetoric—a semantic—that can be codified only after they've been called into question, after the detectors have arrived. Modernist narrative deliberately plays upon the ambiguity and uncertainty such detectors create, upon the lack of privilege assigned to realistic narrative now that its conventional nature has been revealed. Still, realistic narrative is tenacious; that it survived the onslaught of modernism even in an altered state testifies to its strength. Indeed, one of the great modernist texts, Gide's *Les faux-monnayeurs*, is an homage to realism and to the great nineteenth-century novel, though at the same time it questions realism's privilege. Strouvilhou, Gide's counterfeiter, not only counterfeits coins, but wants to edit a literary magazine that will "demonetize fine feelings, and those promissory notes which go by the name of *words*." The *sign* itself must be effaced by emptying it (demonetizing it) as the dadaists did (whose representatives appear in the novel), or by creating signs that are obviously and openly cheap imitations of representations, parodies of the real, gilt on glass (instead of solid

Epilogue

gold coins)—signs that fade almost immediately with use and
that themselves thus come to represent the counterfeit nature
of all representations. As Strouvilhou's patron the Count de
Passavant says, "words only fade when they're printed."

Still, it is impossible for counterfeit things to represent the
counterfeit nature of all representations, since this would im-
ply that counterfeit things are themselves privileged representations. Therefore they can represent only themselves. "If we
manage our affairs well," Strouvilhou says, "and leave me
alone for that, I don't ask for more than two years before a
future poet will think himself dishonoured if anyone can understand a word of what he says." Thus the notion that art is
counterfeit leads to the notion not that art is a fraud or an
inauthentic representation, but that representation itself is
simply not possible, at least in the naive realist sense, the sense
that assumes a clear link between the representation and the
thing represented, so that the latter shines through the former.
The magazine Passavant eventually publishes displays on its
cover a print of the Mona Lisa with a bold moustache drawn
on her face, an oddly historical reference to an actual magazine
cover executed by Marcel Duchamp in 1919.[5] Oddly historical because in this respect, at least, Gide's novel is pho-
tographically realistic: such a cover existed, even if it existed
in order to discredit all representations, photographic or otherwise. In fact Gide himself is parodying the dadaists by treat-
ing them as a historical phenomenon; he even places one of
their progenitors, Alfred Jarry, in a scene in his novel, in
much the same way that novelists like Doctorow today place
historical figures in their texts. Strouvilhou is no spokesman
for Gide, or rather he is a spokesman for the demonic monkey
inside Gide (that fierce moralist) that the author enjoys letting
out now and then to crank up the engine of his novel. Gide
knew that the genuine and the counterfeit are linked by a

[5]Duchamp titled his piece "L.H.O.O.Q." It was the cover of the dadaist
periodical *391*, no. 12, March 1920.

dynamic interplay, not by the kind of triumphant succession Strouvilhou envisions. Counterfeit representations are imitations of other representations and thus apparently bracket the question of reality. But reality takes its revenge: in the glass coin whose gilt rubs off, in the worn paper and faded ink of a bill that may or may not be genuine. The transient nature of counterfeit signifiers is itself a symbol of the stubborn resistance the real offers to all representations. But the power of the counterfeit derives precisely from the credit we give to representations, from our faith that they touch the actual. Without such faith, counterfeiting would be impossible.

And this brings us full circle. The notion that art is counterfeit discredits all representations; yet counterfeiting itself affirms the real, though it also makes it clear that representations are thus a matter of credit or faith. Gide's intention was not to discredit representations; he certainly did not conceive of his own novel as counterfeit. He wanted to bring us through the dizzying oscillations of counterfeit and genuine, representation and reality, to a nearly religious sense that the artist's fidelity to the real is beyond choice, is something that chooses him. For all the counterfeiters in the novel, reality still manages to assert its ontological priority, chiefly in the image of Boris's death, which functions as a kind of irreducible fact, something that cannot quite be processed even by Edouard's fictions. "I shall not make use of little Boris's suicide for my *Counterfeiters*," he says in his last journal entry. "I have too much difficulty understanding it. And then, I dislike police court items. There is something peremptory, irrefutable, brutal, outrageously real about them. . . . I accept reality coming as a proof in support of my thought, but not as preceding it." This *indecency* of reality—as Edouard calls it—is inscribed into the text by the gap that opens up between Edouard and Gide, who does of course make use of Boris's suicide. That is, the novel has its cake and eats it too: it becomes simultaneously the absence and the presence of what it represents. It becomes its own devil, who "is affirmed in our negation," to quote from Gide's journal of his novel. "The more we deny him, the more reality we give him." This is the counterfeiter's project too: by denying the real, he affirms it.

These are not simply clever little paradoxes; all are centrally related to the novel's theme of counterfeiting, of the credit or trust we give to representations, and ultimately of the dialectical relationship between fiction and reality. The subject of Gide's novel is clearly stated within it: "the rivalry between the real world and the representations of it which we make to ourselves." His subject is fiction, as in so many modernist texts; but it is also reality, as in all realist texts. In *Les faux-monnayeurs* the two (fiction and reality) are connected by a necessity whose repeated expression is the disruption of one by the other.

And this is the secret link between realism and modernism. The two movements—like the two centuries—are continuous in more ways than is generally recognized. As we have seen repeatedly in realism, from *Persuasion* to *The Wings of the Dove*, reality in the novel operates as a disruptive force, as a kind of stubborn inertia that resists being taken up by the languages of fiction and domesticated, though, like Gide, most of the novelists we have looked at find ways to inscribe this resistance into the text. If modernism is more self-conscious in its treatment of the representations we make of the world, more insistent upon its apparent dissociation from reality, still this aspect of it was prefigured by the most recurring and most significant obsession of realistic fiction, money—that is, by money as a chimera, a fiction. But the point is that this was only one side of money, whose dream was always eroded by the real, by that which resists desire. So the same dialectic defines both kinds of novels: the rivalry between the world and the representations we make of it.

Only when we see reality as something subsumed under the category of the fantastic do the real differences between the most characteristic twentieth- and nineteenth-century novels appear, because only then does the site of the struggle shift to a reality conceived of as unmediated by society. In my view, *Hunger* is the beginning in the nineteenth century of what has become truly unique in twentieth-century fiction: the representation of ordinary reality as a hallucination. So, Joyce has more in common with, say, Dickens than with Kafka; in both Joyce and Dickens we can sense the rhetoric of fiction, its worked-up surfaces, simultaneously subverting and being subverted by the inertia of physical reality. And Kafka has more in common with Hamsun than with Joyce; both Kafka and Hamsun revert to a transparent mimetic language, but only because their subject is the nearly inconceivable intersection of the subjective and the material. In other words their subject is the prior appropriation of the real by anxiety and hysteria, by an indeterminacy with all the authority of history.

Index

Accident, 64, 129. *See also* Chance;
Contingency
Arbus, Diane, 80
Aristocracy, 33, 40, 75–76, 137–138.
See also Gentry; Leisure
Aristotle, 77, 133
Ashton, T. S., 32–33, 107
Austen, Jane, 41, 44, 101, 113, 139;
Emma, 56–57, 86; *Mansfield Park*, 53,
56–57; *Persuasion*, 8, 21, 24, 45–47,
49, 51–64, 76, 86, 92, 99, 134, 154,
169; *Pride and Prejudice*, 48, 54, 56;
Sanditon, 57; *Sense and Sensibility*, 53,
55–57
Axton, William, 103

Bacon, Francis, 27–28
Balzac, Honoré de, 21, 52, 54, 66, 69,
72, 76–80, 82, 92, 107, 109–110,
112–114, 118, 122, 138, 197; *La
Cousine Bette*, 25, 37, 61, 78, 86–87,
95, 116, 123, 132–141; *Eugénie Grandet*, 35, 65, 77, 79; *Illusions perdues*,
35, 67, 77–79, 123, 152, 157; "M.
Gobseck," 35, 39, 68, 117, 141; *Les
paysans*, 35, 50–51; *La peau de chagrin*,
37–38, 70, 94, 118, 124; *Le Père
Goriot*, 27, 35, 71, 99, 118, 124, 198;
Splendeurs et misères des courtisanes, 77,
140
Bank of England, 15, 31–32
Bank of France, 34
Banks, 31–33, 38

Barthes, Roland, 79, 86, 93–94
Beckett, Samuel, 8–9, 36, 76, 81, 109,
171
Bellow, Saul, 194, 200
Benjamin, Walter, 23, 85, 109–110,
126, 146
Berryman, John, 197
Bills of exchange, 29, 31–32
Boccaccio, Giovanni, 88
Bolingbroke, Henry, 48
Booth, Bradford, 187
Braudel, Fernand, 27–33, 35, 43, 48,
75
Brontë, Emily, 48
Brown, Norman O., 110, 114
Butler, Samuel: *The Way of All Flesh*,
25, 35, 40, 143, 156

Camus, Albert, 93
Capitalism, 19–20, 22, 30, 38, 59, 64,
66–67, 73–74, 142–143, 154, 163,
167, 188–189; history of, 28–29, 31–
32; in *Germinal*, 147–148; in
Nostromo, 149–150. *See also* Banks;
Credit; Debt; Labor; Money
Cervantes, Saavedra Miguel de: *Don
Quixote*, 70, 102
Chance: in the novel, 117–124; in *La
Cousine Bette*, 139–140; in *The
Gambler*, 126–131; in *Hunger*, 163,
170. *See also* Accident; Contingency;
Gambling
Cheever, John, 200

Index

Index

Melville, Herman, 200; *The Confidence
    Man*, 25, 98, 124, 202–203; *Moby
    Dick*, 145, 198
Miller, Henry, 171
Miller, J. Hillis, 20, 25, 68
Mimesis: in fiction, 19, 96–98
Misers, 34–39, 42, 79, 105–106, 109.
    See also Spendthrifts
Mississippi Company, 34, 38
Monaghan, David, 57
Monetary crises, 25
Money: of account, 67; attitudes to-
    ward, 27–30; and democracy, 45–46,
    195; and desire, 118; as excrement,
    18, 36, 79; as a fiction, 20, 66–69,
    72–73, 78–79, 199–200, 206; and la-
    bor, 147–148, 150, 153, 163, 172–
    177, 187; and land, 43–44, 47–56;
    and leisure, 173–177; and marriage,
    44–47, 58–60, 63, 181; and material
    reality, 65–67, 69–73, 77–78; and
    moral worth, 59, 62–63, 66, 70–71,
    195–196; paper, 7, 13–22, 30, 35,
    37–41, 67–68, 78–79, 96–98, 112,
    200; paper, history of, 29–34; and
    religion, 70, 119–120; as representa-
    tion, 7–9, 15–19, 22, 33, 35, 68–69,
    78–79, 96–98, 203–205; and sex, 91;
    and the sordid, 61–63, 68, 70–72,
    75, 172–177, 179–181, 183–185; and
    time, 110–114, 116–117, 124, 126; in
    the twentieth century, 8–9, 171,
    194–196, 198–200. *See also* Credit;
    Debt; Gold; Wealth
Moore, George, 144
Morris, William, 151
Morrison, Arthur, 144
Mortgages, 42, 44, 47, 49–50, 54
Murphy, Brian, 25, 31

Nabokov, Vladimir, 85
Naturalism, 76, 144, 148, 152
Necessity: in fiction, 111–113, 117–
    123, 125–131, 133, 138, 140, 164,
    170
Newton, Sir Isaac, 66
Nobility. *See* Aristocracy; Gentry
Norris, Frank, 144, 160; *McTeague*, 36,
    65, 68–69, 82, 147–148, 157
Novel, the, 25, 84–88; beginnings of,
    108–109; chance in, 117–124, 126–

131, 139–140; closure in, 109–111,
    116, 120–121; dialogue in, 100–101,
    130; eavesdropping in, 84, 87–96,
    98–99, 101–103, 133, 140; of man-
    ners, 8; and material reality, 65–83;
    modern, 8–9, 22, 194–207; necessity
    in, 111–113, 117–123, 125–131, 133,
    138, 140; and paper money, 7, 17–
    18, 20–22, 96–98; plot in, 118–141;
    secrets in, 85–88, 133–135; social
    mobility in, 66, 71–76; time in, 109–
    117, 124–126. *See also* Fiction; Natu-
    ralism; Plot; Realism; Representation

Objects: in fiction, 7, 65–69, 76–81,
    157–158, 165–166, 169–171, 179,
    183–185. *See also* Material reality
O'Connor, Frank, 100, 174

Paper money. *See* Money, paper
Peacock, Thomas Love, 16, 30, 112
Phenomenology, 23–24
Pickpocketing: in fiction, 13, 15–16
Plot, 7, 107, 118–141
Postan, M., 43
Poverty, 143–144, 157–160, 162–166,
    172–173, 176, 180–181, 184–186,
    196. *See also* Labor; Wealth
Prévost, Abbé, 87
Primogeniture, 45
Proust, Marcel, 9, 93, 109, 127, 195
Pushkin, Alexander, 108
Pynchon, Thomas, 76

"Rapunzel," 91–92
Realism, 7–8, 17–18, 20–25, 74, 76,
    123, 189, 198; and the fantastic,
    200–201; and material reality, 65–83;
    and modernism, 201, 203–207;
    nature of, 19, 65, 88, 93–103, 140;
    separation of self and world in, 82,
    84, 98–103, 118. *See also* Novel, the;
    Plot; Representation
Reeve, Robin M., 32–33
Representation: in fiction, 7–9, 17–19,
    22, 96–98, 203–206. *See also* Money,
    as representation; Novel, the;
    Realism
Rexroth, Kenneth, 147
Richardson, Samuel, 116
Rilke, Rainer Maria, 94

Library of Congress Cataloging in Publication Data

Vernon, John, 1943–
   Money and fiction.

   Includes index.
   1. Fiction—19th century—History and criticism.   2. Realism in
literature.   3. Money in literature.   I. Title.
PN3499.V47   1984   809.3′912   84–12166
ISBN 0-8014-1728-7